MASSACHUSETTS PATRIOTS

Their Lives, Contributions, and Burial Sites

JOE FARRELL • LAWRENCE KNORR • JOE FARLEY

SUNBURY
P R E S S ®

Mechanicsburg, PA USA

Published by Sunbury Press, Inc.
Mechanicsburg, Pennsylvania

SUNBURY
PRESS
www.sunburypress.com

For information about special discounts for bulk purchases, please contact Sunbury Press Orders Dept. at (855) 338-8359 or orders@sunburypress.com.

To request one of our authors for speaking engagements or book signings, please contact Sunbury Press Publicity Dept. at publicity@sunburypress.com.

FIRST SUNBURY PRESS EDITION: April 2025

Set in Adobe Garamond | Interior design by Crystal Devine | Cover by Lawrence Knorr | Edited by the authors.

Publisher's Cataloging-in-Publication Data
Names: Farrell, Joe, author | Farley, Joe, author | Knorr, Lawrence, author.
Title: Massachusetts patriots : their lives, contributions, and burial sites / Joe Farrell Lawrence Knorr Joe Farley.
Description: First trade paperback edition. | Mechanicsburg, PA : Sunbury Press, 2025.
Summary: The individuals from Massachusetts who played prominent roles in the founding of the USA are detailed.
Identifiers: ISBN 979-8-88819-355-6 (softcover).
Subjects: HISTORY / United States / Revolutionary Period (1775-1800) | BIOGRAPHY & AUTOBIOGRAPHY / Political.

Designed in the USA
0 1 1 2 3 5 8 13 21 34 55

For the Love of Books!

Contents

Introduction

When most people think about the American Revolution, Massachusetts usually comes to mind first, and then all the events in Pennsylvania and other places. It was in Massachusetts that the Boston Massacre occurred, years before the American Revolution began, introducing us to John Adams, the defense attorney. It was in Massachusetts that the Sons of Liberty led the Tea Party in Boston Harbor in protest of taxes. It was in Massachusetts where the first shots were fired at Lexington and Concord. It was in Massachusetts where Paul Revere made his legendary ride immortalized by Henry Wadsworth Longfellow. It was in Massachusetts where the Patriots did not fire until they saw "the whites of their eyes" at the Battle of Bunker Hill. This was also where Joseph Warren gave his life in battle and Henry Knox brought the cannons to the Dorchester Heights, all the way from Fort Ticonderoga in New York during the Winter, forcing the British to abandon Boston. So, it is easy to say that the Revolution began here.

But we do not lead off with John Adams, as many would likely expect. While the Adams family is intertwined in most of this history, John Hancock was the preeminent figure from Massachusetts, as a two-time President of Congress and the first and third governor of the state. John Hancock was the leader of the rabble in Philadelphia rebelling against King George III at the time of our Declaration of Independence. It was John Hancock who took the most risk, writing his name so large that "King George could read it without his spectacles." It was Hancock leading the Congress when Benjamin Franklin quipped, "We must all hang together, or assuredly we shall all hang separately."

Of course, the Adams family is covered thoroughly. John contributed mightily to the founding of the Federal government in many ways and his wife, Abigail, represented the "better halves" of the Founders, albeit from afar. Cousin Samuel Adams was also integral as a leader of the Sons of Liberty.

This volume includes a wide span of military contributions during the American Revolution, from the travels of Joseph Plumb Martin as a common soldier; to the hidden contributions of Deborah Sampson Gannett, one of the several women who impersonated male soldiers; to officers like the resourceful Henry Knox, the brave Joseph Warren, and the regal Benjamin Lincoln.

Other figures who played important roles are also included, from our first historian, Mercy Otis Warren, to President of Congress Nathaniel Gorham, to our first Commander in Chief, before George Washington, Artemas Ward.

All told twenty-one great Patriots from Massachusetts fill the pages of this book. While they are not close to the total of all persons who sacrificed or contributed in some way to the cause, they represent those most prominent or famous or who gave the most.

Please enjoy the retelling of our founding through the brief biographies of these citizens of Massachusetts. Always remember: "Poor is the nation that has no heroes, but poorer still is the nation that having heroes, fails to remember and honor them." (attributed to Marcus Tullius Cicero)

Lawrence Knorr, Ph.D.
March 2025

John Hancock
(1737 – 1793)

The Signature

Buried at Granary Burial Ground,
Boston, Massachusetts.

—————◆·—————

Articles of Confederation • Declaration of Independence

John Hancock must have been an unusual and remarkable person. He inherited enormous wealth, was educated, nice looking, popular, living a wonderful life, and yet he was willing to risk it all in the cause of the American Revolution. He contributed immensely to our nation's founding in many ways, including serving in the Continental Congress, twice as President of Congress, and as a signer of the Declaration of Independence. His signature on that document was so bold that when people sign their names, they are said to have written their "John Hancock."

—————◆·◆—————

John Hancock was born on his family's farm in Braintree, now Quincy, Massachusetts, on January 23, 1737. His father, John, was a minister and died when young John was seven. He was adopted by his uncle Thomas Hancock, one of Boston's wealthiest merchants, and his aunt Lydia (Henchman) Hancock. Young John lived in an elegant mansion on Beacon Hill called Hancock Manor and was sent to the elite Boston Latin School. He graduated in 1750 and enrolled in Harvard. He received his bachelor's degree from Harvard in 1754 at the age of 17. He then entered his uncle's shipping business. In 1760 he moved to England while building relationships with customers and suppliers. He returned in 1761 and soon became

John Hancock

a partner in the company, House of Hancock. When Thomas Hancock died of a stroke in August 1764, John inherited the business, Hancock Manor, two or three slaves, and thousands of acres of land, becoming one of the colonies' wealthiest men. The slaves were eventually freed through the terms of Thomas's will. John developed a reputation for generosity, but his lavish lifestyle had its critics, including Sam Adams.

In 1765 the British Parliament enacted the Stamp Act tax on the colonies, and it was a catalyst for John Hancock. He became involved in politics protesting regulations like the Stamp Act and Townshend Act. He commandeered public acts of protest and joined in support of a boycott of British goods. To avoid British taxes, Hancock allegedly began smuggling goods aboard his vessels. This made him very popular among the locals, and in 1766 he was elected to the Massachusetts House of Representatives.

Hancock came into direct conflict with the British in 1760, when one of his merchant ships, the *Liberty*, was seized in Boston Harbor by

British customs officials who claimed Hancock had illegally unloaded cargo without paying the required taxes. Being a popular figure, the seizure of his ship led to angry protests by residents. He was taken to court and given a huge fine. It was not the first time Hancock had friction with the Customs Board. Many thought they harassed Hancock because of his politics. He hired John Adams to defend him, and eventually, the charges were dropped without explanation. His guilt or innocence is still debated. Hancock became a local hero for standing up to the British authorities. One result of all this was Hancock and Sam Adams emerged as political partners. Adams was a rabble-rousing firebrand who was hated by the British. He and Hancock, along with James Otis, Paul Revere, and others, formed a grassroots group named the Sons of Liberty. Thus, Hancock became increasingly involved in the movement for American independence, and Massachusetts was at the center of the movement. Boston was dubbed the "Cradle of Liberty."

A result of all the unrest in Boston was a show of military might. Four regiments of the British army were sent to Boston to support the royal officials. The tension between the soldiers and civilians led to what became known as the Boston Massacre in March 1770, in which five civilians were killed and six wounded by British troops. Hancock headed a committee that met with Governor Thomas Hutchinson and demanded the removal of British troops from Boston. He claimed that there were 10,000 armed colonists ready to retaliate if the troops did not leave. The troops being in a precarious position were moved to Castle William, and Hancock was celebrated as a hero reflected in his near-unanimous reelection to the House of Representatives.

Boston became a volatile site once again with the passage of the Tea Act of 1773. Although Hancock did not participate in the Boston Tea Party, he was present at the December 16, 1773, meeting preceding the dumping of the tea and approved of the action. On March 5, 1774, Hancock delivered an important speech on the Boston Massacre's fourth anniversary, denouncing British troops' presence in Boston and questioning Britain's authority over the colonists' lives. The speech was published and widely distributed, enhancing Hancock's stature as a leading Patriot.

In May of 1774, Governor Hutchinson was replaced by Thomas Gage. Whereas Hutchinson tried to win over Hancock, believing that he was too influenced by Sam Adams, Gage took a hard line against both men. In December 1774, Hancock was elected president of the Massachusetts Provincial Congress, which declared itself an autonomous government. Later that month, he was chosen as a delegate to the Second Continental Congress, which served as the colonies' governing body.

Hancock was in the middle of several of the most important events of early American history. He was in Lexington, Massachusetts, on April 18, 1775, when Paul Revere rode his horse to warn fellow colonists that the British were on the move toward Boston. Hancock was with Sam Adams when they heard the alarm. Both men were targeted for arrest by the British. The advance warning allowed them to flee and ultimately escape and make their way to Philadelphia to attend the Continental Congress that convened on May 10. On May 24, Hancock was elected as the third President of the Continental Congress.

When the congress adjourned in August, Hancock made his way to Fairfield, Connecticut, where he wed his fiancée, Dorothy (Dolly) Quincy, on August 28. John and Dolly would have two children, Lydia, who died at ten months, and John George Washington Hancock, who died at nine from a head injury while ice skating.

Hancock was President of Congress when the Declaration of Independence was adopted and signed. He was the first person to sign the historical document and did so with a large, flamboyant signature. According to legend, he signed largely and clearly so that King George could read it without his spectacles.

In October 1777, Hancock told the Continental Congress that he would be resigning the presidency and returning to Massachusetts for health reasons. He had fallen out of favor with both Adamses, who disapproved of Hancock's vanity and extravagance. Many doubted he resigned for health reasons. He rejoined Congress in June 1778, and on July 9, joined representatives from seven other states in signing the Articles of Confederation and then returned to Boston.

Hancock had his chance for military glory shortly after when he led nearly six thousand soldiers to recapture Newport, Rhode Island, from the British. It was a complete failure. He suffered some criticism for the failed attempt but emerged with his popularity intact.

The monument to John Hancock.

After returning to Massachusetts, Hancock desired to stay in the public eye. As the state needed funds to pay soldiers and purchase weaponry, he used his personal funds to assist in these areas. He also handed out food and firewood to the poor at his own expense. According to biographer William Fowler, "John Hancock was a generous man and the people loved him for it. He was their idol."

The new Massachusetts constitution, which Hancock helped frame, went into effect in October 1780. He was the first democratically elected Governor of Massachusetts in a landslide, garnering over ninety percent of the vote. He remained governor until his surprise resignation in 1785. He again cited health reasons, but some critics claim he wanted to avoid a difficult situation. Historian James Truslow Adams wrote that Hancock's "two chief resources were his money and his gout, the first always used to gain popularity and the second to prevent his losing it." The turmoil Hancock avoided was Shay's Rebellion, which his successor, James Bowdoin, had to deal with. In 1786, after nearly two years out of office, Hancock ran again and defeated Bowdoin and pardoned all the rebels. Hancock was reelected to annual terms as governor for the remainder of his life.

He did not attend the 1787 Constitutional Convention but did preside over Massachusetts's 1788 convention to ratify the constitution and gave a speech in favor of it. Even with the support of Hancock and Sam Adams, the convention narrowly ratified it by a vote of 187 to 168.

In his ninth term as governor, he reconciled with his old friend Sam Adams and in his final election as governor, Adams served as his running mate and as lieutenant governor.

In 1789 Hancock was a candidate in the first U.S. Presidential election. He received four electoral votes out of a total of 138 cast. Following a lengthy illness, John Hancock died at his home with his wife at his side on October 8, 1793, at 56 years of age. After a lavish funeral, he was laid to rest in the Old Granary Burying Ground in Boston, where the Boston Massacre victims are also buried. A large obelisk-shaped stone marks his grave.

Abigail Adams
(1744—1818)

Mrs. President

Buried beneath the First Unitarian Church,
Quincy, Massachusetts.

———·•·———

Thought Leader

Abigail Adams had a way with words. She was unique for her time. Without the benefit of any formal education, she was a forward thinker, an early advocate for women's rights, a vital confidant and advisor to her husband, the President of the United States, mother of John Quincy Adams, the sixth president, and the first First Lady to occupy the White House. She wrote many letters to her husband which were preserved and today serve to document much of the Revolutionary War home front and the Continental Congress. She is particularly famous for her March 1776 letter to John Adams and the Continental Congress, requesting they "remember the ladies, and be more generous and favorable to them than your ancestors. Do not put such unlimited power into the hands of the husbands. Remember all men would be tyrants if they could. If particular care and attention is not paid to the ladies we are determined to foment a rebellion, and will not hold ourselves bound by any laws in which we have no voice or representation." Extraordinary sentiment for the times. When John expressed some concern about George Washington's motives Abigail wrote: "If he was not really one of the best-intentioned men in the world, he might be a very dangerous one." John frequently sought the advice of Abigail on many matters and their letters are filled with intellectual discussions on government and politics.

Portrait of Abigail Adams by Jane Stuart after Gilbert Stuart,
circa 1800.

———◆———

Abigail Adams was born Abigail Smith in Weymouth, Massachusetts on November 11, 1744. Her father, William Smith, was a Congregationalist minister and had a large private library. She was educated at home and the library was a big advantage. She was a straight-laced young lady who did not sing, dance, or play cards. For amusement, she read and wrote letters to friends and relatives. John and Abigail were third cousins and had known each other since childhood but around 1762 their relationship took a turn toward romance. Their courtship was slow. They were married by her father on October 25, 1764, when she was nineteen and he was just shy of twenty-nine. In the next twelve years, she gave birth to six children including future president John Quincy Adams.

After their reception they rode off on a single horse to their new home, the small cottage John had inherited. Later they moved to Boston, where his law practice expanded. In 1774, John moved the family to Braintree because the situation in Boston was increasingly unstable. In 1774 John went to Philadelphia to serve as his colony's delegate to the First Continental Congress. Abigail stayed home and the separation began a lifelong correspondence between them forming a rich archive of their relationship and a chronology of the public issues debated and confronted by the new nation's leaders. It is believed that over the years they exchanged over 1100 letters.

As the Declaration of Independence was being debated at the Second Continental Congress Abigail began to press the argument in her letters that the creation of a new form of government was an opportunity to make the legal status of women equal to men. These are some of the earliest known writings calling for women's equal rights. John listened but she was never able to convince him.

As the separation lasted through the revolution Abigail was responsible for raising the children and running the farm and took responsibility for the family's financial matters. All of which she did very well. In 1778 John was named as minister to France and then in 1785 was named the first U.S. minister to England. Until she joined him in 1783, she kept him informed of domestic politics while he confided international affairs to her. When she joined him in Europe she was at first intimidated by the novel experience of Paris but grew to like it. She disliked London where she felt she received a cold shoulder by polite society. One pleasant experience during this time was her temporary guardianship of Thomas Jefferson's daughter Mary (Polly). They formed a deep and lifelong friendship. In 1788 she and John returned to a house in Quincy, Massachusetts which she enlarged and remodeled. It is still standing and open to the public as part of Adams National Historic Park.

When John became Vice President in 1789 Abigail stayed with him in the capital for only part of the time, often returning to Massachusetts to look after their farm and to tend to other business matters. When she was in the capital (New York), she helped First Lady Martha Washington with entertaining dignitaries. John Adams was inaugurated as the second

President of the United States on March 4, 1797, in Philadelphia. Abigail did not attend as she was tending to John's dying mother. She remained a supportive spouse and confidante during his presidency although she incurred a lot of criticism for her involvement with politics. She was accused of advocating war with France, writing pro-administration editorials and asking others to get similar articles published, supporting laws that were unpopular, and promoting public education for women. She did not hesitate to speak her mind which was difficult for some critics to accept. Her political opponents came to refer to her as "Mrs. President."

She was the first First Lady to live in the White House although for only four months, arriving in November 1800. During that time she famously hung her family's laundry in the unfinished East Room to dry. After John's defeat in his presidential re-election campaign, the family returned to Quincy in 1800. Abigail continued to run the farm and care for family members, including their eldest child Nabby who died of cancer at their home in 1814.

For seventeen years, she and John shared time together. She continued a lively correspondence with many people and even resumed writing Thomas Jefferson after hearing of his daughter's death. This also opened a new friendship between John and Thomas Jefferson. She would not live to see her son John Quincy elected President in 1824. She died of typhoid fever on October 28, 1818. She is buried beside her husband in a crypt located in the First Unitarian Church in Quincy. In 1840 her grandson Charles published 114 of her letters and in 1876 he edited the wartime correspondence between John and Abigail.

John Adams
(1735 – 1826)

Second to George

Buried beneath the First Unitarian Church,
Quincy, Massachusetts.

———•◦•———

**Continental Association • Declaration of Independence
Diplomat • Thought Leader • First Vice President
Second President**

John Adams was not a real likable guy. His seemingly inborn conten-
tiousness was a constraint in his political career. Yet he would serve in
both Continental Congresses, sign the Declaration of Independence
after a major role in its writing, serve as the United States' Ambassador
to France, Holland, and Great Britain, and become America's first Vice
President and second President. He made up for his irritating personality
with honesty, competence, and hard work. What he lacked in popularity
he made up in respect. Ben Franklin once wrote about Adams "I am
persuaded that he means well for his country, is always an honest man,
often a wise one, but sometimes, and in some things, absolutely out of
his senses."

He was born in Quincy, Massachusetts in 1735, a fifth-generation
New Englander. His father was a deacon and a town selectman. He was
awarded a Harvard scholarship at age 16 and graduated in 1755 at the
age of 20. His father expected him to become a clergyman but John
chose law instead. In 1764 he married Abigail Smith. The marriage
lasted 54 years and produced six children, one of which (John Quincy
Adams) would become the sixth President in 1825. He made his first

Portrait of John Adams by Gilbert Stuart, circa 1815.

mark politically with his opposition to the Stamp Act in 1765. He wrote articles in the newspapers and gave speeches claiming the act invalid. He soon after moved to Boston and set up his law practice there.

In 1770, Adams agreed to defend eight British soldiers charged with killing 5 civilians in what became known as the Boston Massacre. He justified taking on the very unpopular clients by claiming "It is more important that innocence be protected than it is that guilt be punished, for guilt and crimes are so frequent in this world that they cannot all be punished. But if innocence itself is brought to the bar and condemned, perhaps to die, then the citizen will say, 'whether I do good or I do evil is immaterial, for innocence itself is no protection,' and if such an idea as that were to take hold in the mind of the citizen that would be the end of security whatsoever." Adams won an acquittal for six of the soldiers and the other two, who had fired into the crowd, were convicted of manslaughter. Ultimately this enhanced his reputation as a courageous and fair man.

Adams was elected to the First Continental Congress in 1774 and then to the Second Continental Congress in 1775. In that year he nominated George Washington as commander-in-chief of the Continental Army. Publicly, Adams supported "reconciliation if practicable," but privately agreed with Ben Franklin that independence was inevitable. He opposed various attempts, including the Olive Branch Petition, aimed at trying to find peace between the colonies and Great Britain.

On June 7, 1776, Adams seconded Richard Henry Lee's resolution of Independence and backed it strongly until its passage on July 2. Congress appointed Adams, Thomas Jefferson, Benjamin Franklin, Robert Livingston, and Roger Sherman to draft the declaration. This Committee of Five decided at Adams' urging that Jefferson would write the first draft. Adams played an important role in its completion and it passed Congress on July 4.

Adams was soon serving on as many as ninety committees, chairing twenty-five, more than any other Congressman and in 1777 he became head of the Board of War and Ordnance, which oversaw the Continental Army. Late that same year he was named as commissioner to France and in February 1778 he sailed for Europe. He was to negotiate an alliance with the French who were debating whether or not to recognize and aid the United States. In 1779, Adams was one of the American diplomats to negotiate the Treaty of Paris, which brought an end to the Revolutionary War. After the war, he remained in Europe and from 1784 to 1785 he arranged treaties of commerce with several European nations. In 1785 he became the first U.S. minister to England.

In 1788, Adams returned home after nearly ten years in Europe. The following year, he was placed on the ballot for America's first presidential election. Partly because Adams had been out of the country on diplomatic missions, had not participated in the Constitutional Convention, and had not unduly antagonized anyone in America, he received thirty-four electoral votes coming in second to Washington. In accordance with the Constitution at the time, Adams was sworn in as Vice President. The same results occurred in 1792. Adams' two terms as vice president were

The Adams crypt beneath the United First Parish Church in Quincy, Massachusetts. John is on the left and Abigail on the right.

politically uneventful and he grew increasingly frustrated with the position as he did not have much clout with Washington.

The election of 1796 was the first contested American presidential election. During Washington's two terms, deep philosophical differences had caused a rift and led to the formation of two parties: the Federalists and the Democratic-Republicans. When Washington announced he would not be a candidate for a third term, an intense partisan struggle began. Adams was the Federalist nominee and Jefferson the opponent. Adams won with seventy-one electoral votes to sixty-eight for Jefferson who became vice president. Near the end of his term, he became the first President to occupy the newly constructed White House.

During Adams' term as President, the dominant issue was the threat of war with France who were angered over the Jay Treaty with England. France had supported the Americans during the revolution and now they were at war with England and resented our dealing with them. In response, the French navy began attacking American merchant ships. In 1797, President Adams sent diplomats to create a treaty with France. Upon arrival, three French diplomats, nicknamed "X," "Y," and "Z", proceeded to ask for bribes to start negotiations. The story made its way to the American public and over the next two years, the United States carried on an undeclared naval war with France. Although the country's ships fought many battles, war was never formally declared. To silence critics of the war with France, Congress passed the Alien and Sedition Acts in 1798. These acts were created as a way to punish those who criticize the American government with the intent to harm the government's position. These laws proved very unpopular.

In the election of 1800, Adams again faced Jefferson and Aaron Burr in what was a bitter campaign. The results were Jefferson and Burr receiving 73 electoral votes while Adams received 65. The election tie was decided by the House of Representatives and Jefferson declared the winner. Adams left town in the predawn hours of March 4, 1801, and did not attend Jefferson's inauguration.

Adams and Jefferson reconciled in 1812 and corresponded with each other for years. Adams got to see his son become America's sixth President. Perhaps fittingly, the two Declaration of Independence signatories both died fifty years to the day of the adoption of the document on July 4, 1826. On his deathbed, the ninety-year-old Adams whispered, "Thomas Jefferson survives." It wasn't the case. Five hours earlier, the eighty-three-year-old Jefferson had died at Monticello.

Adams is buried in a family vault beneath the Unitarian Church in Quincy Massachusetts. Unlike Washington and Jefferson, there is no monument to him in the national capital.

Samuel Adams
(1722–1803)

Boston's Radical Revolutionary

Buried at Granary Burial Ground,
Boston, Massachusetts.

Continental Association • Declaration of Independence
Articles of Confederation • Governor

Samuel Adams was an American statesman, political philosopher, and Founding Father, who signed three of the four founding documents. His role in the origins of the American Revolution cannot be overstated. He was a zealot for independence and a thorn in the side of the British. He spoke out against British efforts to tax the colonists and pressured merchants to boycott British products. John Adams, the second President, said of his cousin Sam that he embodied "steadfast integrity" and "universal good character." The Royal Governor of Massachusetts, Thomas Hutchinson, felt differently, saying there existed no "greater incendiary in the King's dominion or a man of greater malignity of heart" . . . as any passionate activist, he was controversial, but for sure, he was an ardent Patriot.

Adams was born in Boston on September 27, 1722. He was one of twelve children born to Samuel Adams Sr. and Mary Adams. Only three of these children lived past the age of three. The parents were devout Puritans, and the family lived on Purchase Street on the south end of colonial Boston. Samuel Sr. was a prosperous merchant, church deacon, and leading figure in Boston politics.

Samuel Adams

Samuel Jr. attended the Boston Latin School and then entered Harvard College at the age of fourteen in 1736. He supposedly was preparing for the ministry but exposure at Harvard to the ideas of philosophers like John Locke, who held that certain rights and liberties were inherent to humanity and that government should reflect the truth, shifted his interest toward politics. He graduated in 1740 but continued as a graduate student, earning a master's degree in 1743. In his thesis, he argued that it was lawful to resist the supreme magistrate if the commonwealth could not otherwise be preserved.

After Harvard, Adams decided to go into business. His business ventures were failures, and finally, his father made him a partner in the family's malthouse. His lack of interest and understanding of business led to its shutting down.

In 1748, Adams and some friends established a political newspaper called *The Independent Advertiser*. Sam became a frequent contributor to this newspaper, which became an outlet for his beliefs. His writings argued that people must resist any encroachment on their constitutional rights.

In October 1749, he married Elizabeth Checkley. Over the next seven years, she gave birth to six children, but only two survived to adulthood. In July 1757, Elizabeth died soon after giving birth to a stillborn son. Adams married again in 1764 to Elizabeth Wells but had no children.

In 1756, he got his first steady job when the Boston Town Meeting elected him tax collector. He often failed to collect taxes and was held liable for the unpaid tax. He often paid with his own funds, and friends often chipped in to bail him out.

The British government was in deep debt after the French and Indian War and passed two measures to tax the colonies. The first, the Sugar Act of 1764, taxed molasses and refined sugar, and Adams was a powerful figure in opposition. He denounced the act, being one of the first to cry out against taxation without representation. Then, in 1765, Parliament passed the Stamp Act, a tax on all legal and commercial documents, newspapers, and court documents. This was like pouring gasoline on a fire and led to the founding of the Sons of Liberty which would play a role throughout the American Revolution. Their motto became "No Taxation without Representation." Adams made frequent use of colonial newspapers and suggested a boycott of British goods. There were frequent riots and violent attacks to intimidate tax collectors. Officials blamed Sam Adams for inciting the violence.

According to the modern scholarly interpretation of Adams, he supported legal methods of resisting parliamentary taxation, such as petitions, boycotts, and nonviolent demonstrations, but opposed mob violence. All the pressure generated by Adams's various activities resulted in the repeal of the Stamp Act in early 1766. The city of Boston rejoiced.

In 1767, Parliament struck again with the Townshend Acts, a series of laws that taxed goods imported to the colonies. The colonists saw the acts as an abuse of power and organized a boycott of British goods. In his letter that became known as the "Massachusetts Circular Letter," Adams urged the other colonies to join in the boycott. In response to protests and boycotts, the British sent troops to occupy Boston and quell the unrest. This resulted in frequent clashes between citizens and troops. In March 1770, after years of agitation, British troops found themselves backed into a corner amid a mob and fired, killing five civilians. Adams called it The Boston Massacre. He wanted the accused soldiers to receive a fair trial, convincing his cousin John Adams to take up their defense. He wanted to demonstrate that Boston was not controlled by a lawless mob. After the defendants were acquitted of murder, however, he wrote a condemnation of the outcome.

In 1772, Adams was behind the formation of the Committees of Correspondence, which connected the town meetings of Massachusetts to one another. Soon similar committees were formed in other colonies as well. In 1773, Parliament passed the Tea Act, which granted the East India Company a monopoly on the tea trade. Sam Adams was a key figure in organizing opposition, resulting in the famous Boston Tea Party in December 1773. His exact role in this event is unsure. Adams never revealed if he went to the wharf or if he was involved in the planning, but he worked to publicize and defend it.

This pain-aggression spiral continued as Parliament responded to the Tea Party by passing a series of four laws in 1774 known as the Coercive Acts or Intolerable Acts. The four acts were intended to punish Massachusetts and send a message to the other colonies. They were the Boston Port Act, Massachusetts Government Act, Administration of Justice Act, and Quartering Act. These oppressive acts sparked strong colonial resistance including the meeting of the First Continental Congress. Adams worked to coordinate resistance to the Coercive Acts, and in June 1774, he proposed the meeting in Philadelphia and was chosen as one of five delegates to represent Philadelphia. Friends bought him new clothes and paid his expenses for his first trip outside Massachusetts.

The Congress met from September 5 to October 26 in Carpenters' Hall with delegates from twelve of the colonies. Georgia did not participate. Sam Adams worked for colonial unity and was a force for the formation of a colonial boycott known as the Continental Association. They agreed to meet again in May. When Adams returned to Massachusetts, he served in the Massachusetts Provincial Congress, which created the first Minuteman companies—militiamen ready for action at a moment's notice. Admiral Montague, the British Governor of Newfoundland and officer in the Royal Navy, upon reading of the events of the Continental Congress, said, "I doubt not but that I shall hear Mr. Samuel Adams is hanged or shot before many months are at end. I hope so, at least."

The Boston Town Meeting selected Adams to attend the Second Continental Congress and added John Hancock to the delegation. Believing rumors that they were to be arrested for treason, Adams and Hancock left Boston in February 1775 and were in Concord on April 19, 1775, when British troops first clashed with local militia, igniting the Revolutionary War. After the battles at Lexington and Concord, General Gage, the commanding officer, issued a proclamation granting a pardon to all who would "lay down their arms and return to duties of peaceable subjects." He, however, excepted Hancock and Adams.

At the Second Continental Congress in Philadelphia, Adams signed the Declaration of Independence. He also nominated George Washington to be Commander in Chief of the Continental Army. His inflammatory rhetoric continued in a speech in Philadelphia where he castigated Americans who sided with the crown. "If ye love wealth better than liberty, the tranquility of servitude than the animating contest of freedom—go from us in peace," he said. "We ask not your counsels or arms. Crouch down and lick the hands which feed you. May your chains set lightly upon you, and may posterity forget that ye were our countrymen." Adams served on military committees in Congress and was particularly concerned with punishing loyalists, i.e., Americans who continued to support the British. He was appointed to the Board of War and was the Massachusetts delegate to the committee appointed to draft the Articles of Confederation. The resulting Articles were sent to the states for ratification in November 1777. Adams urged ratification from Philadelphia, and it was ratified by Massachusetts and signed by Adams in 1778, but it took until 1781 for all states to ratify.

Sam Adams took a two-month break from Congress to return home to Boston and move his family to Dedham, Massachusetts. His home on Purchase Street had been destroyed and vandalized, and all the furnishings had been stolen. He returned to Boston in 1781 after retiring from Congress and never left Massachusetts again.

The remainder of Adams's career was devoted to state rather than national politics. In the 1780s, Adams served as President of the Massachusetts Senate. In January 1788, he was elected to the Massachusetts ratifying convention. He was initially opposed to ratification of the Constitution, but he and Hancock listened to the debate carefully and eventually agreed to support it with the promise that some amendments be added. Even with their support, it barely passed 187 to 168. From 1789 to 1793, he served as Lieutenant Governor under John Hancock. When Hancock died in office, Adams assumed the Governorship. Following that, Adams was elected to three consecutive one-year terms. He retired from politics after his tenure as Governor in 1797. He died at the age of eighty-one on October 2, 1803, and was interred at the Granary Burying Grounds in Boston.

Samuel Adams is a controversial figure in American history. Disagreement about his significance and reputation began before his death and continues to the present. Supporters of the Revolution praised

Grave of Samuel Adams

Adams, but Loyalists viewed him as a sinister figure who used propaganda to incite ignorant mobs. Some on each side claim that without him, there would not have been a revolution. For Adams, personal happiness had never been the supreme goal. He preferred virtue. While other men in Congress and the Army found ways to improve their fortunes, Adams returned to Boston in 1781 even poorer than when he left for the first Continental Congress. Some have dubbed his life as a riches to rags story. He wrote no memoir, resisting even calls to assemble his political writings. He was rare for his ability to keep a secret, any number of which he took to the grave, including the backstory of the Boston Tea Party.

Crispus Attucks
(1723 – 1770)

The Boston Massacre

Buried at Granary Burying Ground,
Boston, Massachusetts.

On March 5, 1770, in the city of Boston, a group of British soldiers were confronted by an ever-growing number of local citizens. The crowd that gathered was angry because one of the soldiers, Private White, had used the butt of his musket to deliver a blow to the head of a young local named Edward Garrick. Tension between the crowd, which continued to draw more Bostonians, and the soldiers continued to grow. Church bells rang out, arousing the curiosity of the locals. Among those joining the crowd was an American of African and Native American descent named Crispus Attucks.

Attucks was born in 1723 in Framingham, Massachusetts. Town histories describe him as a slave of Deacon William Brown. In 1750, Brown took out advertising offering a reward of ten pounds for the return of a runaway slave named Crispus. Whether he was a runaway slave or a free man in 1770 has been long debated by historians.

Attucks worked as a sailor and a whaler, and much of his adult life was spent at sea. On March 5, 1770, he was a member of the crew of a whaling ship that had docked in Boston Harbor. He was scheduled to leave Boston on a ship headed to North Carolina.

Some say that Attucks was the leader of a group of sailors who joined the crowd jeering the British soldiers. As the crowd grew, Private White

Crispus Attucks

believed that reinforcements were needed. As told in *The Boston Massacre: A Family History* by Serena Zabin, the additional soldiers arrived and were led up King Street by Captain Thomas Preston. The street was too narrow for both the crowd and the advancing soldiers. Their bayonets poked people as those gathered attempted to get out of the way. One word many in the crowd agreed they heard was "fire." Was it a command to the soldiers, or was it the taunts of the crowd saying, "You dare not fire." No one knew then, and no one knows now.

One of the witnesses, Jane Crothers, said she saw some in the crowd threatening to kill White as they threw snow, wood and ice at him. She said she heard a civilian ask Preston if he intended to open fire on the crowd. According to Crothers, Preston replied, "Sir, by no means, by no means." She later testified that she saw a man in a dark coat behind the soldiers who encouraged them to fire, saying, "Fire, by God, I'll stand by

"Boston Massacre, March 5th, 1770" by John H. Bufford based on a drawing by William L. Champney, ca.1856 Boston.

you." Again, according to Crothers, the man slapped one of the soldiers on the back, and he opened fire.

Others on the scene told different stories. Thomas Wilkinson. He said he saw nothing being thrown but heard this order given to the soldiers, "Fire, damn your Bloods, Fire." He said at this time the soldiers fired calmly and deliberately. When the dust cleared, five colonists were killed and six others wounded. Attucks took two bullets to the chest and is believed to have been the first to die. His body was taken to Faneuil Hall, where it would lay in state until March 8. At that time, he and the other victims were laid to rest in Boston's Granary Burying Ground. John Hancock and Samuel Adams, among other notable figures, are also buried here. At the time of his death, Attucks was appropriately 47 years of age.

John Adams successfully defended the soldiers who were brought to trial. The man who would become the second President of the United States called the crowd "a motley rabble Of saucy boys, negroes and mo-lattoes, Irish leagues and outlandish Jack Tarrs. Adams charged Attucks with having "undertaken to be the hero of the night," and with having

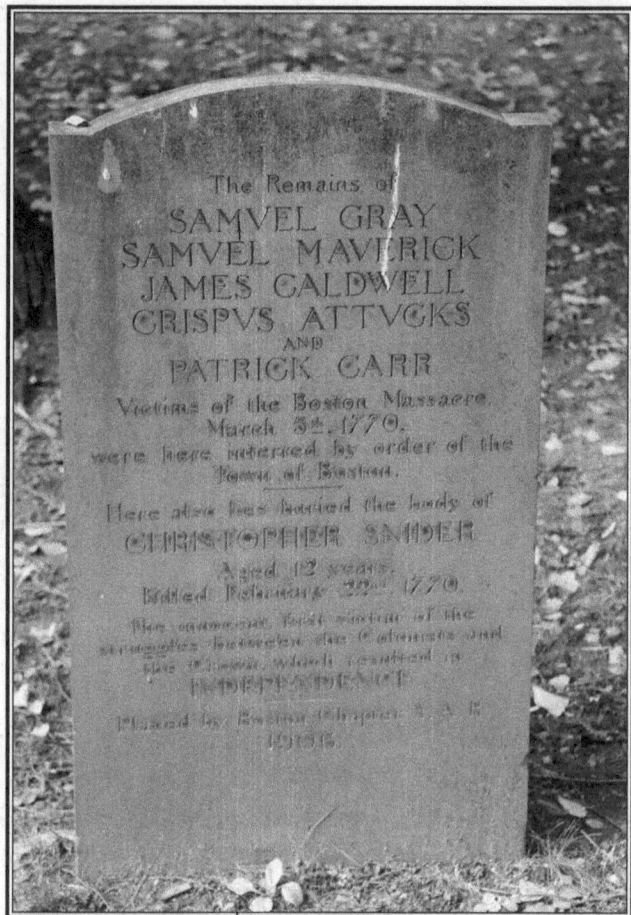

The Remains of
SAMVEL GRAY
SAMVEL MAVERICK
JAMES CALDWELL
CRISPVS ATTVCKS
AND
PATRICK CARR
Victims of the Boston Massacre,
March 5ᵗʰ 1770,
were here interred by order of the
Town of Boston.

Here also lies buried the body of
CHRISTOPHER SNIDER
Aged 12 years,
killed February 22ᵈ 1770.

Grave marker at the Granary Burial Grounds for Crispus Attucks
and others killed in the Boston Massacre.

precipitated a conflict by his "mad behavior." It was Sam Adams, a cousin of John Adams, who named the incident the "Boston Massacre," ensuring the event would not be forgotten.

In 1858, Boston area abolitionists established "Crispus Attucks Day" to commemorate him. Abolitionists at the time pointed to Attucks as a hero of the Revolution and lauded him for playing a heroic role in the history of the United States. In 1886 the spot where Attucks fell was marked by a circle. In 1888, a monument standing 25 feet tall honoring Attucks and the other victims was erected on the Boston Common. In

1940, Attucks was honored with 1 of the 33 dioramas at the American Negro Exposition in Chicago. In 2002, the scholar Molefi Kete Asante listed Attucks as one of the 100 Greatest African Americans. There are multiple schools around the country named in his honor. Martin Luther King Jr. made a reference to Attucks in the introduction to *Why We Can't Wait* As an example of a man whose contribution to history provided a potent message of moral courage.

Thomas Cushing, III
(1725 – 1788)

Protégé of John Hancock

Buried at Granary Burial Ground,
Boston, Massachusetts.

———•———

Continental Association

Thomas Cushing III was a prominent lawyer, merchant, and politician in Boston, Massachusetts. He was elected to the First and Second Continental Congresses and signed the Continental Association. However, he was a voice for reconciliation with England and did not agree with the Declaration of Independence. Regardless, as a protégé of John Hancock, he continued in service of the revolutionary cause.

———•———

Thomas Cushing III was born March 24, 1725, in Boston, Massachusetts, to Thomas Cushing II, a wealthy merchant, and his wife, Mary (née Bromfield). The elder Cushing was active in town politics and as a member of the Old South Church. He also served in the Massachusetts colonial assembly from 1731 to 1747, rising to speaker after 1742. Young Thomas was the second of at least seven children.

Cushing first attended the Boston Latin School before attending Harvard, where he graduated in 1744. He then continued to study law and achieved a master's degree by 1747. Cushing was admitted to the bar and entered the family's merchant business of importing wool products to the colonies. On October 1, 1747, he married Deborah Fletcher, of whom little is known. The number of children from this union is in doubt, with estimates ranging from two to seven.

Thomas Cushing

Following in his father's footsteps, Cushing entered local politics in 1753, winning election as a selectman in Boston, an office which he held for ten years. In 1761, he was elected a member of the Massachusetts General Court, where he served for fourteen years. While frequenting political discussions at Boston taverns, he developed relationships with Samuel Adams and John Hancock. With the latter, a lifelong friendship blossomed, Cushing always supporting the charismatic leader financially and otherwise. While Cushing worked in the background in support of Hancock, he always let his friend take the credit. This led many to see Cushing as little more than a henchman of Hancock.

Following the French and Indian War, when the British were seeking recompense via taxes and duties on the colonies, Cushing, as a merchant, was a loud voice against them, noting the potential negative economic impacts on both sides of the Atlantic. Wrote John Adams of Cushing at the time, "[He] is steady and constant and busy in the interest of liberty and the opposition and is famed for secrecy and his talent for procuring intelligence."

On March 19, 1764, the *Boston Evening Post* reported the election of Thomas Cushing, Samuel Hewes, and Ezekiel Lewis as selectmen for the city of Boston, serving in the Massachusetts Assembly. Cushing, who held the position for ten years, soon rose to Speaker of the Assembly, becoming the most powerful elected politician in the colony, second only to the royal governor. One historian noted Cushing's "charm and wit" led to his annual re-election until the colonial assembly was swept away by the Revolution.

As speaker during the rising tensions in Massachusetts, Cushing played a key role as a frequent correspondent with the royal governor and the assembly's agent in London, Benjamin Franklin. Both agreed to try to moderate the situation at that time, following the Boston Massacre. In 1772, Cushing and Hancock declined to serve on the Boston Committees of Correspondence, maintaining their moderation. At that time, Franklin tried to deflect the blame for the tensions from the British government to Royal Governor Thomas Hutchinson, who was suggesting colonial rights be abridged. Franklin sent letters from royal appointees to that effect to Cushing. He was to show them only to a select few people, but when the radical Samuel Adams got wind of them, he published them in 1773. This caused an uproar, increasing tensions on both sides and calling for Franklin to resign as a colonial agent. Following this public lambasting, Franklin switched firmly to the pro-independence cause. The Boston Tea Party then ensued.

Cushing now reluctantly joined the Committee of Correspondence and denounced the Coercive Acts. When the governor dissolved the assembly, a Provincial Congress was called, and Cushing was a delegate. On June 17, 1774, Cushing, John Adams, Samuel Adams, and James Bowdoin were elected as delegates from Massachusetts to the First Continental Congress in Philadelphia.

Thomas Cushing, III (1725–1788)

In October 1774, General Thomas Gage arrived in Massachusetts and succeeded Hutchinson, establishing military rule over the rebellious colony. Meanwhile, Congress passed the Continental Association, collectively stating their grievances to the King. Cushing penned his name to this document. Cushing was included on the list of radical leaders sent to General Gage because, as speaker, his signature was affixed to all petitions. Gage never detained Cushing. Wrote Cushing to his wife at the time:

> I wish I could write you any politics, but as I am enjoined to secrecy, must refrain. It is currently reported in the city that the Congress have voted that no goods shall be imported from Great Britain and Ireland after the first day of December next, and that none imported after that day shall be used or consumed, and that the Congress have also voted that no goods or merchandise shall, after the 10th day of September next, be exported from the Colonies to Great Britain, Ireland, or the West Indies, unless our grievances shall be redressed before that time, and I do not deny or contradict these reports.

Cushing was reelected to this seat on December 5, 1774; February 6, 1775; and November 1775. He attended the session from September 5 to October 26, 1774; from May 10 to August 2, 1775; and from September 11, 1775, to about January 2, 1776. Cushing continued to urge moderation and was against declaring independence. He continued to believe economic pressure would force England's hand without further conflict and believed the preferred path forward was a colonial union under Great Britain. Other Massachusetts delegates began to distrust him. This cost him his seat in Congress. Elbridge Gerry, who was pro-independence, narrowly defeated him, ending his term on January 31, 1776. This gave the pro-independence camp in Massachusetts a majority. When Cushing returned to Massachusetts from Philadelphia, he continued to work against independence, orchestrating delays in the polling process by which the state would vote for independence.

John Hancock, who was then president of the Continental Congress, then stepped in for Cushing. He made him commissioner of marine affairs, overseeing the procurement of ships for the Continental Navy. For

Thomas Cushing's grave.

several years he was also the chief commissary responsible for supplying Massachusetts troops.

In 1778, Cushing was involved in an unsuccessful attempt to create a new constitution for Massachusetts, which the voters rejected. Perhaps frustrated, in 1779, he declined to be run for the Continental Congress.

In 1780, Cushing was not involved in drafting the new state constitution that was adopted that year. That year, Cushing was appointed as one of the chief commissaries responsible for supplying the French troops at Newport, Rhode Island, a position that permitted him to enrich himself through favorably priced contracts.

Cushing ran for the state senate in 1780 and won. The newly elected senators then selected Cushing as the President of the Senate. However, when Hancock ran for governor of Massachusetts in 1780, Cushing ran with him as lieutenant governor. Both won and Cushing promptly resigned from the senate after only a few weeks. Cushing served as lieutenant governor until 1788, and in 1785, when Hancock had resigned, Cushing was the acting governor until the new governor, James Bowdoin, could take office. Cushing had run for the position himself but lost.

During Bowdoin's second term as governor, Shay's Rebellion broke out in response to his harsh economic policies. Hancock ran against Bowdoin in 1787 and won. Once again, he served with Cushing. In 1788, Cushing was a delegate to the state ratifying convention of the new U.S. Constitution. He also became one of the founders of the American Academy of Arts and Sciences.

Thomas Cushing died suddenly in Boston on February 28, 1788. He was buried in the Granary Burying Ground in Boston. Cushing, Maine, is named after him.

Francis Dana
(1743 – 1811)

Congressman at Valley Forge

Buried at Old Burying Ground,
Cambridge, Massachusetts.

Articles of Confederation • Diplomat

Francis Dana was an American statesman, lawyer, and jurist from Massachusetts. He served as a delegate to the Continental Congress in 1777–1778 and again in 1784. He was a signer of the Articles of Confederation.

He was born on June 13, 1743, in Charlestown, Massachusetts. His parents were wealthy and respectable and gave him the benefit of an excellent education. He graduated from Harvard in 1762 and took up the practice of law. He was admitted to the bar and set up a practice in Boston in 1767. He opposed British colonial policy and became a leader of the Sons of Liberty. He was elected to Massachusetts' provincial congress in 1774. In the spring of 1774, the Continental Congress felt it important to send someone to England to represent the patriots and to ascertain the real feeling among England's rulers. Dana was selected. He was just 31 years old. The question was whether we should seek to adjust our differences with England as its colony or whether we should declare absolute independence. He returned in March 1776 convinced that all hope for a friendly settlement must be abandoned. He threw his whole influence for independence. He impressed his convictions upon the Continental Congress and just over three months after his return they voted for Independence.

Portrait of Francis Dana etched circa 1885.

He was a member of the Massachusetts executive council from 1776 to 1780 and served as a delegate to the Continental Congress from 1776 to 1778. He signed the Articles of Confederation in 1778. In January 1778, Congress appointed him chairman of the committee assigned to visit George Washington at Valley Forge and confer with him about the reorganization of the army. The committee spent about three months at Valley Forge and assisted Washington in preparing the plan of reorganization which Congress in the main adopted. In that same year, he was a member of the committee that considered a peace proposal offered by Lord North of Great Britain, which he vigorously opposed and which Congress rejected.

In 1779, France went to war with England and took the side of the colonists. Congress needed to send able and discreet persons to Europe and selected Dana to accompany John Adams and his son John Quincy Adams. In December 1780, Dana was appointed minister resident to the

Russian court. He was never officially received at the court of Catherine the Great and left Russia in August 1783. After his return, he was again elected to Congress in 1784. He resigned from Congress 1785 to accept a seat on the Supreme Court of Massachusetts.

Dana was named a delegate to both the Annapolis Convention and the Constitutional Convention but attended neither due to poor health. He was, however, a member of the Massachusetts Ratifying Convention. He left there briefly during its proceedings, after a spat with Elbridge Gerry who opposed the ratification.

Dana was appointed Chief Justice of the Massachusetts Supreme Court in 1791, a position he held until his retirement from the bench in May 1806. He became a charter member of the American Academy of Arts and Sciences in 1780.

Francis Dana died at Cambridge, Massachusetts, on April 25, 1811, and is buried in Cambridge's Old Burying Ground.

The Dana family marker at the Old Burying Ground in Cambridge, Massachusetts (photo by Lawrence Knorr).

Deborah Sampson Gannett
(1760 – 1827)

Female Minuteman

Buried at Rock Ridge Cemetery,
Sharon, Massachusetts.

Military

Deborah Sampson Gannett, more commonly known as Deborah Sampson was a Massachusetts woman who disguised herself as a man to serve in the Continental Army from May 1782 to October 1783, during the American Revolutionary War. She is one of a very small number of women with a documented record of military combat experience in that war. She served for seventeen months in the army under the name of Robert Shurtleff (also spelled Shirtliffe and Shurtliff in various sources). She was wounded in battle in 1782 and honorably discharged at West Point in 1783. She was also one of the first women to receive a pension for military service and the first woman to go on a national lecture tour.

Deborah Sampson was born on December 17, 1760, in Plympton, Massachusetts. She was one of seven children born to Jonathan Sampson and Deborah Bradford. Some of Deborah's ancestors included passengers on the *Mayflower*. One of these, Priscilla Mullins Alden, was later immortalized in Longfellow's poem, "The Courtship of Miles Standish."

Jonathan abandoned his family and took up with a woman named Martha in Lincoln County, Maine. Her mother was in poor health and could not provide for the children so they were placed with friends and

Portrait of Deborah Sampson Gannett, artist unknown.

relatives. Deborah, at the age of five, was sent to live with an elderly widow Mary Thatcher. Upon the death of the widow when Deborah was eight, she became an indentured servant in the household of Jeremiah Thomas in Middleborough, Massachusetts. Mr. Thomas had ten sons and as an indentured servant she was bound to serve the family until she was eighteen. She was given food, clothing, and shelter in exchange. She was, however, not sent to school like the Thomas boys because Mr. Thomas did not believe in education for women. She learned by having the Thomas boys review their studies with her each night after her chores were done. She grew to be approximately 5'9" tall when the average at that time was 5' for a woman and 5'6" to 5'8" for a man.

When she turned eighteen, she was released from her indentured servitude and took a job as a schoolteacher. She supplemented her income by spinning and weaving at various homes and at Sproat Tavern, a gathering place for men who discussed the battles of the revolution.

In early 1782, Sampson wore men's clothing and joined an Army unit in Middleborough under the name of Timothy Thayer. She collected a bonus but failed to show up at the appointed time. She had been recognized by a local resident. She paid back a portion of the bonus she hadn't spent and the Army did not punish her. She tried it again in the town of Uxbridge, Massachusetts near Worcester on May 20, 1782, and this time was successful. She used the name Robert Shurtleff and was chosen for the Light Infantry Company of the 4th Massachusetts Regiment. Light infantry companies were elite troops, specially picked because they were taller and stronger than average. They were referred to as "light" infantry because they travelled with less equipment and supplies and took part in small, risky missions.

Her regiment marched from Worcester to West Point to protect the Hudson Highlands from the British who still occupied New York City. There were numerous skirmishes between the two forces along "no man's land." At one point, Sampson's regiment encountered another American unit headed by Colonel Ebenezer Sproat. She had spent time working at Sproat Tavern owned by the Colonel's father, and feared she would be recognized but was not.

During her first major battle, on July 3, 1782, near Tarrytown, New York she received two musket balls in her thigh and a slash in her forehead from a sabre. She begged her fellow soldiers to leave her alone and let her die, but they refused, put her on a horse, and rode six miles to a hospital. When she arrived, doctors treated her head wound but Deborah did not tell them about her thigh wounds fearful that they would discover her true sex. She limped out of the hospital and removed one of the balls with a penknife and a sewing needle. The second ball was too deep for her to reach. Her leg never fully healed and bothered her for the rest of her life.

She was some time recovering from her wounds before she could rejoin her company. On April 1, 1783, Sampson was promoted and spent seven months serving as a personal orderly to General John Patterson. In June, the Fourth Massachusetts was transferred to Philadelphia. That summer she became ill with a severe fever, rendering her unconscious. She was cared for by Dr. Barnabus Binney who discovered that Robert

Shurtleff was really a woman. He did not reveal his discovery but took her to his house where his wife and daughters and a nurse took care of her.

When she recovered, Dr. Binney asked Deborah to deliver a note to General Patterson. She correctly assumed it would reveal her gender. Patterson notified General Henry Knox who in turn notified General Washington. He ordered her honorably discharged. She received her honorable discharge on October 25, 1783, at West Point after a year and a half of service.

Sampson returned home and on April 7, 1785, married Benjamin Gannett, a farmer from Sharon, Massachusetts. They had three children and adopted one. Life was hard for the Gannetts as the farm was small

Bronze statue of Deborah Sampson Gannett in front of the public library in Sharon, Massachusetts (photo by Lawrence Knorr).

and the land was not productive because it had been worked extensively.

In 1792, Sampson petitioned the
Massachusetts State Legislature for
pay that had been withheld because
she was a woman. The legislature
granted her thirty-four pounds with
interest back to her discharge date.
The order was signed by Governor
John Hancock. At the urging of her
friend Paul Revere, Sampson went
on tour in 1802, capitalizing on
her wartime fame. She lectured in
Massachusetts, Rhode Island, and
New York and was perhaps America's
first woman lecturer. She delivered
a set of speeches about her wartime

The grave of Deborah Sampson Gannett
(photo by Lawrence Knorr).

experiences and at the conclusion of her speech, she would leave the stage
and return in uniform and demonstrate how to clean, load, and fire a
musket. Her audiences were astonished.

In 1804, she petitioned Congress for a pension for her wartime service. Paul Revere wrote a letter in support of her petition. This had never
before been requested by or for a woman. On March 11, 1805, Congress
approved the request and placed her on the Massachusetts Invalid Pension
Roll at the rate of four dollars a month. In 1816, Congress increased her
pension to $6.40 a month.

In 1813, Sampson moved in with her son and daughter-in-law in
Sharon and died there on April 29, 1827, at the age of 66. She was
buried in nearby Rock Ridge Cemetery. Her gravestone is located a short
distance from the hill on which her grandson, George Washington Gay,
erected a monument to her and the Civil War veterans many years later.

The town of Sharon memorializes Sampson with Deborah Sampson
Street, a statue in front of the public library, Deborah Sampson Field,
and the Deborah Sampson House which is privately owned and not
open to the public.

The town of Plympton, Massachusetts has a boulder on the town green with a bronze plaque inscribed to Sampson's memory.

In 1983, Governor Michael Dukakis signed a proclamation which declared Deborah Sampson as the Official Heroine of the Commonwealth of Massachusetts.

Nathaniel Gorham
(1738 – 1796)

President of Congress

Buried at Phipps Street Cemetery,
Charlestown, Massachusetts.

Continental Congress • United States Constitution

Nathaniel Gorham was born in Charlestown, Boston, Massachusetts, on May 27, 1738. He was the son of Captain Nathaniel Gorham, a packet boat operator (a packet boat was a regularly scheduled service carrying freight and passengers), and his wife Mary Soley. His third great grandfather, John Howland, came to America on the *Mayflower* and signed the Mayflower Compact.

He received little formal education but was apprenticed at 15 to Nathaniel Coffin, a merchant in New London, Connecticut. He left Coffin's employ in 1759 and returned to Charlestown and established his own small business there, which quickly succeeded. Four years later, in 1763, he married Rebecca Call, and they had nine children together.

Gorham began his political career as a public notary but was soon elected to the colonial legislature (1771 to 1775), where he emerged as a staunch Patriot. During the revolution, he displayed an exceptional talent for administrating that proved crucial to his state's wartime government. He was selected to serve on the Massachusetts Board of War, which organized Massachusetts' military logistics and manpower (1778–17810). In 1779 he was a delegate to Massachusetts' first constitutional convention. He represented his community in both the upper and lower houses of the new state legislature, serving several times as the lower house speaker.

Nathaniel Gorham

Gorham served as a delegate to the Continental Congress from 1782-83 and 1785-87 and served as its president after the resignation of John Hancock in June 1786. He served as president until November of that year.

In 1786, Gorham was involved in a very controversial matter that became known as the Prussian Scheme. Shay's Rebellion in western Massachusetts convinced many Americans that a stronger, centralized national government was necessary. The shortcomings of the Articles of Confederation were fanning the fears of anarchy. When Massachusetts debtors took up arms, refused to pay their debts, and closed the courts, Gorham predicted worse would follow.

These types of disturbances fueled the movement for convening a convention to modify the Articles of Confederation. Getting consensus to modify the Articles took some time. When the delegates convened in Philadelphia in May 1787, there were widely circulated rumors that the meeting was to offer to enthrone Prince Frederick of Prussia as king of the United States. So intense were the rumors that the convention issued a public denial that any proposal for reestablishing monarchy was being considered. The reason for these rumors was that Gorham, while President of the Continental Congress, wrote to Prince Henry, the younger brother of the Prussian King Frederick the Great, offering to make him king of the United States. Henry's response, found more than a century later, proved what many had assumed was a legend was to decline. He reportedly believed that the American public would not be likely to submit to a king. A letter addressed to Baron von Steuben, dated a few months before the Constitutional Convention, was discovered in the Prussian archives in the early 1900s. It refers to the offer and his refusal. Von Steuben, who was living in New York, was involved in the proposal. Some have attributed the natural-born citizen clause in the US Constitution as an attempt by the Philadelphia Convention to end the persistence of rumors of European royalty being invited to assume a hypothetical US throne.

Gorham was elected as a Massachusetts delegate to the Constitutional Convention in 1787. He played an influential part, frequently speaking, sitting on the Committee of Detail, and serving as chairman of the Committee of the Whole. He pushed for a central government strong enough to protect interstate commerce, promote international trade, and regulate the use of paper money. He favored long presidential and senatorial terms and the appointment of federal judges by the executive. He also wanted a consolidation of military authority through control of the militia by the central government.

To gain support for these things, he was willing to accept southern demands about slavery. Gorham was pessimistic about the future of his state and country. He believed, in the aftermath of Shay's Rebellion, that Massachusetts would divide between east and west over the constitution question and that the country would divide into several independent nations within 150 years.

He signed the Constitution and was a crucial participant in Massachusetts' struggle for ratification. Ratification was won only when Gorham and other Federalists proposed possible amendments to the constitution to attract moderates. The final vote was 187 to 168.

Gorham did not serve in the new government he had helped create. In 1788 he and a friend Oliver Phelps bought 2,600,000 acres in western New York. The deal was a disaster and ruined him financially. By 1790 the two men were bankrupt, which led to a fall from the heights of Boston society and political esteem.

Gorham died in Charlestown, Massachusetts, on January 11, 1796, at the age of 58. He is buried in the Phipps Street Cemetery in Charlestown. Gorham Street in Madison, Wisconsin, and Gorham, New York are named in his honor.

The overgrown grave of Nathaniel Gorham.

Samuel Holten
(1738 – 1816)

Physician Continental Congressman

Buried at Holton Cemetery,
Danvers, Massachusetts.

Continental Congress • Articles of Confederation • U.S. Congress

Samuel Holten was a physician from Salem Village (now Danvers), Massachusetts, who became a long-serving Continental Congressman who signed the Articles of Confederation. He also served in several state positions, including nearly twenty years as a local judge. He was briefly a member of the US House of Representatives in the early republic.

———◆———

Holten was born on June 9, 1738, in Salem Village, Massachusetts, the son of Samuel Holten, Sr., and Hannah (née Gardner) Holten, who was a member of the famous Gardner family of the colony. Holten was descended from his great-grandfather, Joseph Houlton, from Bedfordshire, England, who came to the colonies with his wife, Sarah Ingersoll, of the Connecticut Ingersolls.

Holten attended local grammar schools and then studied medicine under Dr. Jonathan Prince. Upon his certification as a physician, Holten opened a practice in Gloucester, Massachusetts. In 1758, he married Mary Warner with whom he had two daughters.

The young doctor and his family soon returned to Salem Village, where he continued his practice and became very popular. In 1768, he was appointed to the General Court.

Judge Samuel Holten

As tensions began to mount with England, Holten was elected to the Massachusetts Provincial Congress from 1774 to 1775. He was next a member of the Massachusetts Committee of Safety.

Holten was appointed to the Continental Congress on February 10, 1778, to replace John Adams, who had been sent to France. He arrived in York, Pennsylvania, in time to sign the Articles of Confederation on behalf of Massachusetts on March 10, 1778. He was then reelected on October 15, 1778, serving with Samuel Adams, John Hancock, Elbridge Gerry, Francis Dana, James Lovell, and Timothy Edwards through 1779.

In the 1840s, historian Mellen Chamberlain had the opportunity to make notes from Dr. Holten's diary used during the Continental Congress. Some of the entries follow:

1778, June 23. Attended in Congress, and the chief of the day was taken up in disputes on the articles of confederation [sic].

1778, July 11. This day was the first time that I took any part in the debates in Congress. We have accounts of the arrival of a French Fleet in the Delaware. 12 Ships of the line & 4 Frigates.

1778, July 14. I let the Hon. Samuel Adams Esqr. have 400.00, of which he is to pay to James Otis (a minor) being my part of what the delegates of our state have agreed to advance to sd [said] minr. & Mr. Adams is to write to his friends & procure the money, & account with me for the same.

1778, Oct. 7. Met a committee on this evening on General [Benedict] Arnold's accounts.

1778, Oct. 15. A manifesto or Proclamation from Commr. of the British king appeared in the papers of the day, offering a Gen. Pardon, but I believe there is but few people here want their pardon.

1778, Dec. 14. Monday. There was a grand ball at the City Tavern this evening, given by a number of French gentlemen of distinction. I had a card sent me, but declined attending. I think it is not a proper time to attend balls when the country is in such great distress.

Holten was again appointed to the Continental Congress on November 18, 1779, continuing his service until he resigned on July 29, 1780, when he began two years of service in the Massachusetts Senate and the Massachusetts Governor's Council, a role he held off and on for fourteen years. He was again appointed to the Continental Congress on October 4, 1780, but did not attend any sessions in 1781.

On October 4, 1782, Holten was again appointed to the Continental Congress. He served through November 1, 1783. The following year, in addition to his state senate seat, he returned for another term, serving through October 1785. On August 17, 1785, Holten was elected the president pro tempore of the Continental Congress, when President Richard Henry Lee was unable to preside. Holten ran the Congress until the new president, John Hancock was able to attend. During this time, he, Elbridge Gerry, and Rufus King blocked the call for a convention to reform the Articles of Confederation, believing not enough time had passed to judge the effectiveness of it.

In 1786, Holten continued in his state senate seat and was again elected to the Continental Congress, serving until August 9, 1787. Holten changed his mind about the Articles and participated in the Constitutional Convention in Philadelphia in 1787. However, he did not approve of its final form, with a strong central government and lacking a Bill of Rights. He opposed ratification of the Constitution. Meanwhile, he also served in the state House of Representatives and was in attendance at the Massachusetts ratifying convention in 1788.

There, he allied himself with the anti-Federalists and opposed ratification. Unfortunately, Holten became ill at this time and was unable to have the desired impact.

As the Federalists took control of the Federal Government, Holten seemed finished with national politics. He sat in the state Senate in 1789 and 1790 and on the Governor's Council. He twice failed to be elected to the US House of Representatives in 1788 and 1790. He also lost a bid to be appointed to the US Senate in 1790.

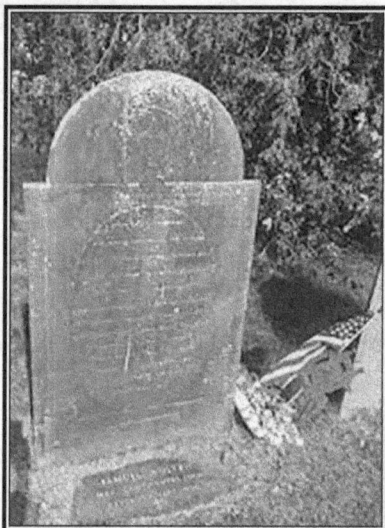

The grave of Samuel Holten

In 1792, Holten finally won his seat in the US House of Representatives, serving in the Third Congress, from 1793 to 1795, representing Massachusetts' First District.

Following his single term, Holten returned to Danvers and served as a judge on the Essex County Probate Court for nearly twenty years, from 1796 to 1815.

In his 77th year, with his health failing, Holten resigned his judgeship in 1815. He died soon after on January 2, 1816. He was buried in the Holten Family Cemetery in Danvers, Massachusetts. His large tombstone reads:

> Erected to the Memory of the Hon. Samuel Holten, Who Died Jan. 2, 1716, aged 78 years. He Sustained Various Offices of Trust, Under the State Government, and That of the Union, With Ability and Integrity, to the Almost Unanimous Acceptance of His Constituents.

The Judge Samuel Holten House remains a historic site in Danvers, Massachusetts.

Henry Knox
(1750–1806)

"Miracle on the Dorchester Heights"

Buried at Thomaston Village Cemetery,
Thomaston, Maine.

Major General • Secretary of War

Henry Knox was a Boston bookseller who became a senior general of the Continental Army during the Revolutionary War. When our fledgling country needed a miracle, he delivered one. In 1775, as the siege of Boston wore on, George Washington placed Knox in command of an expedition to retrieve artillery and supplies recently captured at Fort Ticonderoga on Lake Champlain in New York. Facing barely navigable roads and dangerously inclement weather, Knox made the three-hundred-mile trek north, arriving on December 5, 1775. After recovering the 120,000-pound lot of guns, mortars, and cannons from Ticonderoga, Knox transported the convoy by boat down Lake George and then led a caravan of sleds and oxen to continue the journey overland from the lake's southern end to Boston. He arrived in Boston with the guns on January 27, 1776, just in time to deploy them on Dorchester Heights. The appearance of Knox's guns on the high ground compelled the British Army and Navy to withdraw on March 17, 1776.

Henry Knox's parents, William and Mary, were Scots immigrants who came to Boston in 1729. He was the seventh of ten children. Henry's father was a shipmaster and abandoned the family and died in the West Indies in 1762. Henry had been attending the famous Boston Latin

Major General Henry Knox

School but quit after his father died and apprenticed to a bookbinder to help his family. He had access to many books and read voraciously. He educated himself in many subjects, particularly military strategy and weaponry. He also got involved in Boston's street gangs and became known as one of the toughest fighters in his neighborhood.

Knox's life changed as tensions between the American colonies and Britain escalated. He became an ardent supporter of the Patriot cause, participating in the political protests that culminated in the American Revolution. He was present at the Boston Massacre in 1770 and played an active role in the Sons of Liberty, a secret organization advocating for colonial rights.

In 1772, Knox founded the Boston Grenadier Corps, a local militia unit. In 1773, an accident with a gun cost him two fingers on his left hand. For the rest of his life, Knox would keep his hand wrapped in a handkerchief whenever he was in public.

In 1774, Knox began courting Lucy Flucker, the daughter of one of Boston's most prominent Loyalist families. She was a frequent visitor to his bookstore which he opened in 1771 and was very popular. John Adams was one notable patron. In June of that year, the couple wed despite opposition from her father. Lucy's brother served in the British army. After the war broke out at Lexington and Concord, the couple fled Boston. Her family disowned her after she chose to side with her husband. Their commitment to each other and the American cause would endure throughout the war and beyond.

After they left Boston, Knox volunteered for the Continental Army. His abandoned bookstore was looted, and all its stock was destroyed or stolen. He served under General Artemas Ward and built fortifications around the city. He directed cannon fire at the Battle of Bunker Hill. When George Washington arrived, he was impressed by the work Knox had done. With John Adams' help in the Continental Congress, Knox received a commission as the colonel of the artillery regiment.

As the siege of Boston wore on, Knox suggested that an expedition be sent to capture the cannons and supplies at the recently captured Fort Ticonderoga, New York. Washington agreed to put Knox in charge of the expedition. It became known as The Noble Train of Artillery, as described in the opening paragraph. It was a complete success; not one gun was lost. This pivotal maneuver forced the British to evacuate Boston in March making a significant early victory for the Continental Army. Historian Victor Brooks called the maneuver "one of the most stupendous feats of logistics" of the entire war. Knox's effort is commemorated by a series of plaques marking the Henry Knox Trail in New York and Massachusetts.

After Boston, Washington took his forces to defend New York, and Knox joined the army there. The British forces numbered about 30,000, while American forces numbered about 18,000. The outnumbered Americans were forced to retreat all the way to Pennsylvania on December 8, 1776.

On the evening of December 25, Washington made his famous trip back across the Delaware River, directed by Knox, to surprise the Hessian forces at Trenton, capturing 1000 men and much-needed supplies,

Knox's brigade moving cannons from Ticonderoga to the Dorchester Heights

greatly boosting sagging American spirits. Knox was promoted to brigadier general for this accomplishment and given command of an artillery corps expanded to five regiments. He then participated in the Battles of Princeton, Brandywine, Germantown, and Monmouth. In 1780, Knox sat on the court-martial of Major John André, the British officer who had conspired with American Brigadier General Benedict Arnold to gain British control of West Point. Knox further contributed to the Patriot cause by placing the artillery for Washington during the victorious siege of Yorktown and establishing an artillery school.

Since Cornwallis' surrender on October 19, 1781, Knox had been serving as commander of West Point. The following March, Knox became the army's youngest major general.

With peace at hand, the Confederation Congress began to order the demobilization of the army in April 1783. The next month, in May, Knox founded the Society of the Cincinnati, a fraternal society of Revolutionary War officers that survives to this day. He served as its first Secretary General. After the Treaty of Paris formally ended the war that September, Knox oversaw the withdrawal of British troops from New York. When the last British troops left New York City in November

1783, Knox rode at the head of forces that took over the city and attended Washington's farewell address to his officers at Fraunces Tavern. As Washington completed his speech, Knox was the first officer to come up and embrace Washington with a hug and tears. With Washington's resignation, Knox held the post of senior officer in the army.

In March 1785 the Confederation Congress appointed Knox the nation's second United States Secretary of War. He served in that position until Washington was elected President and appointed him as Secretary of War under the new constitution in 1789. As Secretary, he supported plans for a national militia, supervised the initial steps of forming a regular navy and managed conflicts with many groups of native peoples.

Knox's grave

In January 1795, Knox was forced to resign due to rumors that he had profited from contracts for frigates to fight pirates. Washington accepted his resignation with regret. Knox and his family settled on an estate at Thomaston, Massachusetts (now Maine), which he called Montpelier. During this period, Knox reportedly gained a lot of weight, approaching nearly 300 pounds. On October 22, 1806, he swallowed a chicken bone that lodged in his throat and caused an infection. He died three days later, on October 25, at age 56. He was buried on his estate with full military honors. Numerous towns, cities and military installations bear his name, most notably Fort Knox, Kentucky.

Benjamin Lincoln
(1733 – 1810)

Received the Surrender at Yorktown

Buried at Old Ship Burying Ground,
Hingham, Massachusetts.

Major General • Secretary of War

Benjamin Lincoln was a Major General during the American Revolution who participated in and was present at three major surrenders: Saratoga, Charleston, and Yorktown. As the war was ending, Lincoln became the first Secretary of War for the new nation. He also led the suppression of Shay's Rebellion in Connecticut. Lincoln was not related to the future sixteenth President of the United States, Abraham Lincoln.

Lincoln, born January 24, 1733, in Hingham, Suffolk County, Massachusetts, was the first son and sixth child of Colonel Benjamin Lincoln and his second wife, Elizabeth (née Thaxter) Lincoln. The elder Lincoln was descended from Thomas Lincoln, a cooper who was one of the community's first settlers. He was also one of the wealthiest men in Suffolk County, owning vast amounts of land, and served on the governor's council from 1753 to 1770. Colonel Samuel Thaxter, Lincoln's maternal grandfather, was also an influential citizen and helped to settle the boundary with Rhode Island in 1719.

Young Lincoln attended local schools and worked on the family farm and then established his own farm. At age 21, in 1754, he became the town constable. The following year, he joined the 3rd Regiment of

Benjamin Lincoln

the Suffolk County Militia under his father, the colonel. At age 23, in 1756, Lincoln married Mary Cushing, the daughter of Elijah Cushing of Pembroke, Massachusetts, who was also from an old Hingham family. Over the years, the couple had eleven children, seven of whom survived to adulthood.

In 1757, Lincoln was elected the town clerk of Hingham and held the post for twenty years. He also remained in the militia throughout the French and Indian War but saw no action. In 1763, he was promoted to major.

After the war, in 1765, Lincoln was elected town selectman in Hingham. He held this post for six years. During this time, he protested the new taxes imposed by Parliament and the Boston Massacre, making him a leading force among the Patriots in Hingham. In 1772, Lincoln was elected to represent the town in the provincial assembly. He was also promoted to Lieutenant Colonel of the 3rd Regiment of the Suffolk Militia.

In 1774, General Thomas Gage arrived as the Governor of Massachusetts. He officially dissolved the assembly, but it reconstituted itself as the Massachusetts Provincial Congress. Lincoln was elected to this body and oversaw militia organization and supply. Following the nearby Battles of Lexington and Concord in April 1775, Lincoln was appointed to the Congress's Committee of Safety and was elected to the executive council, governing Massachusetts outside occupied Boston. As the Continental Army was forming, Lincoln was involved in securing supplies, ammunition, and gunpowder, reinforcing the siege and buying time until Gage and the British left Boston upon the arrival of Henry Knox's cannons.

Lincoln was promoted to Major General of the Massachusetts Militia in January 1776. He was responsible for defending Massachusetts following the British evacuation. He and General Artemas Ward of the Continental Army led the defense of the state and improved fortifications. That May, the last Royal Navy ships were expelled from Boston Harbor.

With the aging of Artemas Ward, Lincoln saw an opportunity for promotion and lobbied for a Continental Army position. While this was not forthcoming, he was sent with some militia to assist General George Washington in his defense of New York in August 1776. While in Connecticut, Lincoln was ordered to prepare an expedition across Long Island Sound to raid British forces on Long Island. However, Washington retreated, and the mission was aborted. Lincoln was then ordered to assist in securing the retreat of the Continental Army at White Plains, New York. There, his regiments joined the main Continental Army during the Battle of White Plains in October.

With enlistments expiring, Lincoln returned to Massachusetts to gather new recruits. Obviously, Washington was impressed with Lincoln because, on February 14, 1777, he was promoted to Major General in the Continental Army. Washington described him in his letter to Congress as "a gentleman well worthy of notice in the Military Line."

Two months later, on April 13, 1777, Lincoln led an engagement against the British and Hessians at Bound Brook, New Jersey. The enemy attempted a surprise attack on Lincoln's headquarters, which was only three miles from British sentries. Outnumbered 5,000 to 400, Lincoln barely escaped without being captured.

That summer, in July, British General John Burgoyne threatened northern New York from Quebec, via the Hudson River. Washington sent Generals Lincoln and Arnold and Colonel Morgan to assist General Philip Schuyler, who was subsequently replaced by Horatio Gates. Lincoln and his 2,000 troops were ordered to harass the British supply lines as they moved south. Unfortunately, the leader of the New Hampshire Militia, John Stark, would not cooperate, refusing to be under the control of the Continental Army due to a previous promotion snub. Instead, Stark, in mid-August, led his troops to victory at the Battle of Bennington, capturing or killing 1,000 Hessians from Burgoyne's army.

Next, in September, General Gates ordered Lincoln and his men to join him and assigned him to hold the eastern side of the Hudson River. Lincoln arrived on September 22, following Colonel Morgan's decisive victory at Freeman's Farm, where his sharpshooters killed most of the offices and three-fourths of the artillerymen. They captured six of ten British cannons.

During the Battle of Bemis Heights on October 7, which occurred on the west side of the Hudson, Lincoln's troops saw no action. During the battle, General Arnold was struck in the leg during a charge, even though General Gates had relieved Arnold of command due to insubordination.

Afterward, Lincoln's forces pushed the British back further. He recommended heading off the British at the ford at Fort Edward before they could return to Fort Ticonderoga. Gates agreed, and while enacting the plan, Lincoln's forces engaged in a skirmish and Lincoln was struck in the ankle by a musket ball. He was transported to Albany and treated. There, he learned of Burgoyne's surrender on October 17. Lincoln was bedridden for months, returning to Hingham with his son's help in February 1778. Lincoln's right leg was shorter for the rest of his life. When Arnold's seniority was restored, Lincoln was the lowest-ranking major general, but he decided not to resign over the slight.

Lincoln was back in the saddle in September 1778 when Washington made him the Commander of the Southern Department, replacing Major General Robert Howe. This was a very large and independent command. Lafayette and "Light Horse Harry" Lee were also assigned to Lincoln, opposing Clinton and Cornwallis on the British side.

The following year, in the spring, Lincoln led an attack on the British at Augusta, Georgia, but this left Charleston open to attack. In October, the French under Lincoln, including 500 free Black Haitian soldiers, led a siege of Savannah, Georgia, which failed, resulting in over 1,000 American and French casualties. Lincoln's forces retreated to Charleston, South Carolina, where they garrisoned. The British seized this opportunity in March 1780, devastating Patriot properties in the low country and laying siege to Charleston. Morale was low in South Carolina, but Governor Rutledge convinced Lincoln to fight on. However, when Lincoln requested 1,000 enslaved African Americans to be armed to help fend off the British, the South Carolina legislature declined and permitted the British to pass through South Carolina. Without any Continental Navy support and against superior forces, Lincoln was soon forced to surrender over 5,000 men to General Sir Henry Clinton on May 12, 1780, but some Continental forces and the South Carolina Militia escaped. Lincoln was captured but denied the honors of war in surrender. He was then paroled and sent back to General Washington.

Washington did not give up on Lincoln. Next, he made him second-in-command for the Yorktown Campaign. He led a large portion of the army from Head of Elk, Maryland, to Hampton, Virginia, and then west to Yorktown. After the French helped trap the British on October 19, 1781, General Lord Charles Cornwallis surrendered but feigned illness rather than appear at the surrender ceremony. He sent Irish General Charles O'Hara to do the deed. Washington, insulted by Cornwallis's behavior, had O'Hara surrender to General Lincoln instead, avenging his previous mistreatment.

As the Revolution was ending, under the new Articles of Confederation, Lincoln was made the nation's first Secretary of War, serving from 1781 to 1783. He was succeeded by Major General Henry Knox. Lincoln was also elected to the American Academy of Arts and Sciences in 1781 and was one of the original members of the Massachusetts Society of Cincinnati, selected as its president on June 9, 1783. Ten days later, he supported the election of George Washington as the President General of the order.

In rebellion against tough economic policies following the war, some angry citizens in western Massachusetts, led by Daniel Shays, attempted to seize an armory and overthrow the state in 1787. Benjamin Lincoln, leading 3,000 privately funded militia, led the suppression of the revolt. Known as Shay's Rebellion, this action was one the leading events to trigger the need for a new federal constitution. Lincoln was a strong supporter for the creation of this reform and voted in support of it as a delegate from Suffolk County, Massachusetts. The state ratified the Constitution on February 6, 1788.

During the first presidential election, on February 4, 1789, Lincoln was one of twelve men who received electoral votes, receiving the vote of one elector from Georgia.

Later in life, Lincoln was active in public affairs, serving as Massachusetts's Lieutenant Governor for a term and the lucrative position of Boston's Port Collector for many years. In 1806, when the elderly Lincoln tried to resign as the Collector, President Thomas Jefferson requested that he stay until a successor was found. Representative Josiah Quincy III then tried to have Jefferson impeached in January 1809, even though he was set to leave office in only two more months. Lincoln finally retired in 1809 and passed in Hingham on May 9, 1810.

During Lincoln's funeral, the bells in Boston and other nearby towns were tolled for an hour, and the flags of vessels and at forts and navy yards were flown at half-mast. Pallbearers at his funeral included John Adams, Cotton Tufts, Robert Treat Paine, Richard Cranch, and Thomas Melvill. Lincoln was buried in the Old Ship Burying Ground behind the Old Ship Church in Hingham, Massachusetts.

Lincoln was largely forgotten in the years after the Revolution despite being part of the victories at Saratoga and Yorktown and the defeat at Charleston, though he is shown in the famous painting *The Surrender of Cornwallis* by John Trumball that hangs in the US Capitol.

Grave of Benjamin Lincoln

Typically, towns named Lincoln in the South are named for him as opposed to Abrahan Lincoln. Examples include counties and or towns in Alabama, Georgia, Kentucky, Missouri, North Carolina, and Tennessee. Lincoln in Vermont and Lincolnville in Maine are also named for him, as are streets in Columbia, South Carolina, and Savannah, Georgia. Lincoln Hall at the U.S. Coast Guard Training Center in Yorktown, Virginia, bears his name.

In 1972, Benjamin Lincoln's lifelong home in Hingham, Massachusetts, was declared a National Historic Landmark.

James Lovell

(1737 – 1814)

Teacher, Orator, Signer, Spy

Buried at Unknown Location.
Windham, Maine.

———◆◆◆———

Continental Congress • Signer of the Articles of Confederation

James Lovell was a teacher from a Loyalist Boston family who was imprisoned by the British for spying. Upon his release, he was immediately elected to the Continental Congress, representing Massachusetts. Lovell signed the Articles of Confederation. Despite participating in the Conway Cabal and believing George Washington to be "overrated," President Washington appointed him to a lucrative Customs House position in Boston after the Revolution.

———◆◆◆———

Lovell was born in Boston, Massachusetts, on October 31, 1737. He was the son of John Lovell, headmaster of the Boston Latin School, and his wife, Abigail (née Green). The elder Lovell graduated from Harvard in 1728. Ten years later, he succeeded Dr. Nathaniel Williams as the headmaster of the school where young James, Samuel Adams, and John Hancock received their preparatory education.

James also attended Harvard, graduating in 1756. He then worked with his father at the Latin School. In 1759, James earned a Master of Arts from Harvard, continuing with his father until the school closed in April 1775, as the Siege of Boston was underway.

James and his father were close during these early years. In 1760, James married Mary Middleton, with whom he had more than ten

James Lovell

children, nine of whom survived to adulthood. Lovell also became a noted orator. One such speech was delivered at Boston's Old Faneuil Hall to a massive crowd following the Boston Massacre in April 1771. Lovell's father was not pleased with the speech. Said James, "The horrid bloody scene we here commemorate, whatever were the causes which concurred to bring it on that dreadful night, must lead the pious and humane of every order to some suitable reflections. The pious will adore the conduct of that Being who is unsearchable in all his ways, and without whose knowledge not a single sparrow falls, in permitting an immortal soul to be hurried by the flying ball, the messenger of death, in the twinkling of an eye, to meet the awful Judge of all its secret actions."

Lovell continued to deviate from his father's Loyalist leanings and joined with patriots James Warren, Josiah Quincy, and the Adams cousins, Samuel and John, in demanding increased freedoms from England.

However, Lovell did not openly participate in the Boston Tea Party or the First Continental Congress. He wrote from Boston on May 3, 1775:

> Mrs. Lovell has suffered extremely in the Head, fears a fixed Disorder there, but is I hope only suffering thus thro Weakness. My Family is yet w[ith] me. Children are prepared to go away, and Mrs. Lovell w[ith] the rest will follow when able, if I so judge proper. I am not yet ripe to determine, I shall tarry if 10 Seiges [sic] take place. I have determined it to be a Duty which I owe the Cause & the Friends of it, and am perfectly fearless of the Consequences. An ill Turn, of a most violent Diarhea [sic], from being too long in a damp place, has contirm'd Doctr Gardners [sic] advice to me not to go into the Trenches, where my whole Soul lodges nightly. How then can I be more actively serviceable to the Friends who think with me, than by keeping disagreeable post among a Set of Villains who would willingly destroy what those Friends leave behind them.

When the body of James Warren was searched by the British after the Battle of Bunker Hill on June 17, 1775, documents were found written in James Lovell's hand showing British troop movements. Ten days later, Lovell's home was searched, and additional documents were found confirming he was a spy for the rebels. He was taken into custody and jailed in Boston. Lovell spent nine months in Boston's stone jail until the British left, at which point he was taken to Halifax, Nova Scotia, where he was imprisoned with Ethan Allen for another nine months. While Lovell could have been executed for spying, he was only imprisoned. Curiously, his father, the Loyalist, followed him to Nova Scotia and later died there in 1778. There is no record of the elder Lovell appealing to the British to spare his son, but the scenario is very likely.

Lovell must have made an impression on his friends in Boston who were in Congress and also with the new commander of Continental forces, George Washington, to whom he had written about his imprisonment. Wrote Washington on December 19, 1775:

Inclosed [*sic*] is a letter I lately received from Mr. James Lovell. His case is truly pitiable. I wish some mode could be fallen upon to relieve him from the cruel situation he is now in. I am sensible of the impropriety of exchanging a soldier for a citizen: but there is something so cruelly distressing in regard to this gentleman, that I dare say you will take it under your consideration.

While the letter from Lovell no longer survives, it also made an impression upon Congress, noting Lovell maintained "under the severest trials the warmest attachment to public liberty, and an inflexible fidelity to his country." Congress agreed to an exchange of Major Andrew Skene, a British prisoner, for Lovell. Washington noted it in a letter to Jonathan Trumbull on September 23, 1776.

Months after being freed, Lovell was elected to a seat in the Continental Congress on December 10, 1776, joining John Hancock, Samuel Adams, John Adams, Robert Treat Paine, Elbridge Gerry, and Francis Dana as representatives from Massachusetts. Lovell was the only Continental Congressman to be "continuously present" for five contiguous years through 1781. Lovell served on the Committees of Foreign Correspondence and Secret Correspondence. He was known for his ciphers, which were impossible to crack without the key, though Ben Franklin tried.

During the summer of 1777, following the loss of Fort Ticonderoga to the British, Lovell was a supporter, along with Dr. Benjamin Rush, of General Horatio Gates to take command of the army. Gates had just taken over the Northern Department from Philip Schuyler. Washington managed to survive the intrigue known as the "Conway Cabal" to remain as the commander-in-chief.

Lovell seems to have been closest to John and Abigail Adams, frequently corresponding with them. He especially seemed close to Abigail when John was in France. He wrote Abigail, whom he called by a pet name, "Portia," wondering what John was doing with his private time in France. The letters were flirtatious in nature.

Lovell signed the Articles of Confederation on July 9, 1778. During this time, Lovell was part of a group known as the anti-Gallicans, who feared a subordinate relationship with France and desired a more open relationship with all of Europe. Among them were Francis Dana, the Adams cousins, and the Lees of Virginia. They were suspicious of Ben Franklin's actions at Versailles. They were also behind sending Dana as Minister to Russia in 1780.

During the Revolution, Lovell's oldest son, James, served as a low-level officer in the Continental Army. He saw action at the Battle of Monmouth and served under "Lighthorse Harry" Lee in the Southern Campaign. He was wounded several times.

Following his service in Congress, Lovell returned to teaching. He also was a tax collector in Massachusetts in the 1780s. Despite their prior differences, President Washington appointed Lowell to a customs position in Boson in 1789, holding the position for the rest of his life.

On July 14, 1814, while visiting his friend, Reverend Peter T. Smith, at Windham, Maine, James Lovell died. He was 86. His burial location remains lost.

Lovell's grandson, Joseph Lovell, was the first Surgeon General of the USA, serving from 1818 to 1836. A connection to *Apollo 13* commander James Lovell has not been proven.

Joseph Plumb Martin
(1760 – 1850)

Private Yankee Doodle

Buried at Sandy Point Cemetery.
Stockton Springs, Maine.

Military

Joseph Plumb Martin was a Connecticut militiaman and member of the Continental Army who served mostly in the Northern Theater during the American Revolution. He was lost to history until his detailed memoir from 1830 was rediscovered in the 1950s, providing a priceless primary source for the day-to-day experiences of the common soldier.

Martin was born on November 21, 1760, in Becket, Massachusetts, the son of Reverend Ebenezer Martin and his wife, Susannah (née Plumb) Martin. His father was Yale-educated and from a well-to-do family.

When young Joseph was seven years old, he was sent to live in Milford, Connecticut, with his affluent grandparents. Milford was ninety miles south of Becket, on the Long Island Sound. Here, Martin received a well-rounded education, including reading and writing.

On April 19, 1775, the Battle of Lexington and Concord occurred near Boston, Massachusetts, harkening "The Shot Heard 'Round the World." Young Joseph, approaching his 15th birthday, wanted to fight with the rebels, but his grandparents resisted the idea. When Joseph threatened to run away and join an American privateer to fight the British Navy, they relented and allowed him to join the Connecticut Militia. He enlisted in June 1776, aged fifteen, as a private.

Martin's first tour of duty took him to the New York City area, serving under George Washington, at the start of the British Long Island Campaign. This was disastrous for the Americans, highlighted by Washington's escape across the East River to Manhattan in the fog on August 19, 1776. Martin participated in the Battles of Harlem Heights and White Plains before his tour ended in December 1776, just before Washington's crossing of the Delaware River and the Battles of Trenton and Princeton. Instead, Martin returned to his grandparents in Connecticut.

Joseph Plumb Martin photograph

The following spring, still itching to join the fight, Martin joined the Continental Army on April 22, 1777, and served until the end of the war. He was initially assigned to the 17th Continental Regiment, formerly the 8th Connecticut Regiment, under Brigadier General James Mitchell Varnum.

In 1777, Martin participated in the Siege of Fort Mifflin near Philadelphia and the Battle of Germantown prior to encamping at Valley Forge for the winter.

The following year, Martin was assigned to the Light Infantry and was promoted to corporal. He participated in the Battle of Monmouth that summer.

In 1779, Martin camped with Washington at Morristown. During the summer of 1780, Martin was promoted to sergeant and was assigned to the Corps of Sappers and Miners upon recommendation from his superior officers. He then witnessed John André being escorted to his execution that fall.

At the decisive Battle of Yorktown during the fall of 1781, Martin's unit was the vanguard for Alexander Hamilton's regiment, digging parallel entrenchments and clearing the field of defenses before Hamilton's capture of Redoubt #10. Martin's account of the action:

At dark the detachment was formed and advanced beyond the trenches and lay down on the ground to await the signal for advancing to the attack, which was to be three shells from a certain battery near where we were lying. All the batteries in our line were silent, and we lay anxiously waiting for the signal. The two brilliant planets, Jupiter and Venus, were in close contact in the western hemisphere, the same direction that the signal was to be made in. When I happened to cast my eyes to that quarter, which was often, and I caught a glance of them, I was ready to spring on my feet, thinking they were the signal for starting. Our watchword was "Rochambeau," the commander of the French forces' name, a good watchword, for being pronounced Ro-sham-bow, it sounded, when pronounced quick, like rush-on-boys.

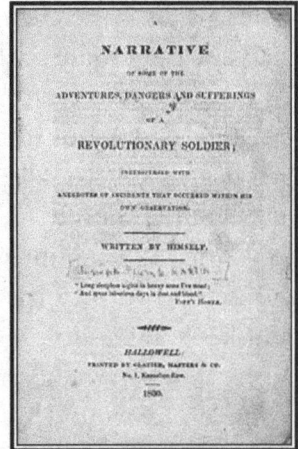

Martin's memoir

We had not lain here long before the expected signal was given, for us and the French, who were to storm the other redoubt, by the three shells with their fiery trains mounting the air in quick succession. The word up, up, was then reiterated through the detachment. We immediately moved silently on toward the redoubt we were to attack, with unloaded muskets. Just as we arrived at the abatis, the enemy discovered us and directly opened a sharp fire upon us. We were now at a place where many of our large shells had burst in the ground, making holes sufficient to bury an ox in. The men, having their eyes fixed upon what was transacting before them, were every now and then falling into these holes. I thought the British were killing us off at a great rate. At length, one of the holes happening to pick me up, I found out the mystery of the huge slaughter.

As soon as the firing began, our people began to cry, "The fort's our own!" and it was "Rush on boys." The Sappers and Miners soon cleared a passage for the infantry, who entered it rapidly. Our Miners were ordered not to enter the fort, but there was no stopping them. "We will go," said they. "Then go to the d———," said the commanding officer of our corps, "if you will." I could not pass at the entrance we had made, it was so crowded. I therefore forced a passage at a place where I saw our shot had cut away some of the abatis; several others entered at the same place. While passing, a man at my side received a ball in his head and fell under my feet, crying out bitterly. While crossing the trench, the enemy threw hand grenades (small shells) into it. They were so thick that I at first thought them cartridge papers on fire, but was soon undeceived by their cracking. As I mounted the breastwork, I met an old associate hitching himself down into the trench. I knew him by the light of the enemy's musketry, it was so vivid. The fort was taken and all quiet in a very short time. Immediately after the firing ceased, I went out to see what had become of my wounded friend and the other that fell in the passage. They were both dead. In the heat of the action, I saw a British soldier jump over the walls of the fort next to the river and go down the bank, which was almost perpendicular and twenty or thirty feet high. When he came to the beach he made off for the town, and if he did not make good use of his legs, I never saw a man that did.

Following the victory at Yorktown, Martin accompanied Washington's army back to New York and was discharged in June 1783, before the British evacuated and the Continental Army mustered out that fall.

Next, Martin taught school in New York before settling on Maine's frontier as one of the founders of the town of Prospect, near modern-day Stockton Springs. There, in 1794, he married Lucy Clewley (born 1776). The couple had five children, including Joseph, born 1799; Nathan and Thomas, twins born 1803; James Sullivan, born 1810; and Susan, born 1812.

Also in 1794, Martin's modest 100-acre farm was embroiled in a dispute with former Major General Henry Knox, who as a land speculator, claiming 600,000 acres in what is now known as Waldo County, Maine. Martin's farm was within this claim, and Martin sued to be able to farm his land.

In 1797, Knox's claim was upheld, and Martin's land was appraised at $170, payable over six years in three installments of either cash or farm products. Martin had no money and begged Knox to keep the land, but the general ignored him. However, there is no record of Knox even responding to Martin, and Martin stayed on his land, farming only eight acres.

Over the years, Martin became well-known locally as a farmer, selectman, justice of the peace, and town clerk, a role he held for over twenty-five years.

General Knox died in 1806 and never demanded payment from Martin. However, by 1811, his farmland was reduced to fifty acres and then to nothing in 1818, when he appeared in Massachusetts General Court with other veterans seeking his pension. Martin then received $96 per year for the rest of his life.

Knowing other veterans were having difficulty achieving their pensions, as the nation passed its fiftieth birthday since the Declaration of Independence, Martin began writing about his experiences to call attention to their service. He had written stories and poems over the years, but in 1830, he completed a memoir based on his now-lost journals. This memoir, entitled *A Narrative of Some of the Adventures, Dangers, and Sufferings of a Revolutionary Soldier, Interspersed with Anecdotes of Incidents that Occurred Within His Own Observations*, was published anonymously in Hallowell, Maine, but received little attention. In 1835, the Federal government began offering pensions to enlisted soldiers or their surviving families.

In 1836, on the sixtieth anniversary, a platoon of United States Light Infantry, passing through Prospect, Maine, learned of Plumb and his location. They stopped outside his house and fired a salute in honor of the seventy-five-year-old veteran.

Martin died on May 2, 1850, at age 89. He was buried at the Sandy Point Cemetery, near Stockton Springs, Maine, next to his wife.

In the 1950s, a copy of Martin's book was donated to the Morristown National Historical Park. Little, Brown then published a new edition in 1962 under the title *Private Yankee Doodle*. Other editions have followed with various introductions and forewords by famous historians.

Often cited by scholars and used by re-enactors, Martin's memoir is also critiqued for potential bias or embellishment. However, he does convey in detail the daily experiences of the common soldiers, especially at difficult times such as the winter at Valley Forge.

Martin has since been portrayed in various television documentaries about the American Revolution. Copies of his first edition book reside at the Library of Congress, the US Army Military History Institute at Carlisle, Pennsylvania, and at the Morristown National Historical Park. The Valley Forge National Historical Park has a trail named in his honor that encircles the park.

Martin's grave

James Otis Jr.
(1725 – 1783)

"Founding Firebrand"

Buried at Granary Burying Ground,
Boston, Massachusetts.

Pamphleteer • Thought Leader

James Otis Jr. was an attorney, legislator, political activist, and pamphleteer from Boston who was an early thought leader in the ultimate pursuit of independence from Great Britain. A mentor of Sam Adams and inspiration for John Adams, Otis is credited with coining the phrase "taxation without representation is tyranny." A Freemason, Otis was also an abolitionist who lobbied for freedoms and rights for all regardless of race. Otis was unable to participate more actively in the Revolution due to his declining mental health and alcoholism.

Otis was born on February 5, 1725, in West Barnstable, Massachusetts, the second of thirteen children of Colonel James Otis Sr. and his wife, Mary (née Allyne) Otis. The elder Otis was a militia officer and attorney. Brothers Joseph and Samuel and nephew Harrison Gray Otis were leading Patriots in the Revolution. Otis's sister, Mercy, married James Warren, and the two were active in the Patriot cause. Mercy was also a satirist and historian.

Throughout his youth, Otis disappointed his father, who expressed this in letters and urged his son to find religion to better himself. Instead, Otis attended Harvard to study law, beginning at age 14. He graduated in

James Otis Jr.

1743 and quickly rose to prominence in Boston as a defense lawyer, successfully defending pirates in Nova Scotia and young men in Plymouth accused of rioting on Guy Fawkes' Day.

In 1755, Otis married a wealthy merchant's daughter, Ruth Cunningham. She had inherited over £10,000, so Otis tolerated their political differences, complaining she was a "High Tory." According to John Adams, Otis said, "She was a good Wife, and too good for him."

Despite the tensions, the couple had three children: James, who lived to age 18; Elizabeth, a Loyalist like her mother who married a British Army captain; and Mary, who married Major General Benjamin Lincoln of the Continental Army.

Otis's first controversy in court occurred in 1760 when Governor Francis Bernard appointed him the Advocate General of the Admiralty Court. However, Otis resigned when the governor reneged on appointing his father as the Chief Justice of the Massachusetts Superior Court and instead appointed Thomas Hutchinson, a longtime rival.

Soon after, Otis represented several Boston businessmen who challenged the Massachusetts Writs of Assistance, permitting local officials to search and confiscate property without cause. In the Superior Court, during *Paxton v. Gray* in 1761, Otis argued against the writs, stating "An Act against the constitution is void . . . and if an act of Parliament should be made . . . the executive courts must pass such acts into disuse."

In a five-hour oration before the State House in February 1761, he continued the fight before five red-robed judges while a young John Adams listened. Said Otis of the Writs of Assistance, "It appears to me the worst instrument of arbitrary power, the most destructive of English liberty . . . that was ever found in an English law book." Otis was unsuccessful in changing the law. However, he did gain the notice of those present and became known as an early revolutionary, especially for labeling the King and Parliament as oppressors of the colonists. Bostonians elected him to the Massachusetts House of Representatives, where he was a member of the Stamp Act Congress.

Recalled John Adams, years later, "Otis was a flame of fire; with a promptitude of classical allusions, a depth of research, a rapid summary of historical events and dates, a profusion of legal authorities . . . Then and there was the first scene of the first Act of opposition to the Arbitrary claims of Great Britain. Then and there, the Child Independence was born. . . . The seeds of Patriots & Heroes . . . were then & there sown." Sections of Otis's 1761 speech were used and enhanced by John Adams over the years.

In 1762, Otis published his first political pamphlet, *A Vindication of the Conduct of the House of Representatives*, where he first uses an example of unsanctioned expenditures by the legislature.

In 1764, Otis published a pamphlet, *The Rights of the British Colonies Asserted and Proved*, that expanded upon his earlier arguments, stating that rights are granted from nature and God rather than from the government and that the purpose of government was for the good of society and not the pleasure of monarchs. He added that the colonies lacked representation in Parliament, and thus, it was unconstitutional for Parliament to tax them, stating: "The very act of taxing, exercised over those who are not represented, appears to me to be depriving them of one of their most essential rights." He also argued for racial equality, stating, "The colonists are by the law of nature freeborn, as indeed all men are, white or black."

By this time, Otis was seen as a firebrand. Lord Mansfield said of his pamphlet, "It is said the man is mad. The book is full of wildness." Friends referred to him as *Furio*, Latin for "in a rage." Rival Hutchinson called him "The Great Incendiary." Wrote John Adams in his diary, "his imagination flames, his passions blaze; he is liable to great inequalities of temper; sometimes in despondency, sometimes in a rage."

Otis's beliefs regarding Natural Law were further described in his 1765 pamphlets, *Considerations on Behalf of the Colonists* and *Vindication of the British Colonies*, espousing equal representation in the government. However, he mysteriously reversed himself in the pamphlet "*Brief Remarks on the Defence of the Halifax Libel*," in which he admitted Parliament had complete authority over the colonies. Some believe this erratic behavior was either to set a potential defense against treason or he had become mentally ill. Regardless, it was Otis's last pamphlet.

Contemporaries noted the mental decline of Otis in the 1760s, and his relationship with his wife was strained. Wrote John Adams in his diary about Mrs. Otis, "She gave him certain lectures."

In 1769, as tensions rose in Boston, Otis worried that "The times are dark and trying. We may soon be called on in turn to act or to suffer." That summer, outraged at a slanderous article about him, Otis threatened to "break the head" of tax commissioner John Robinson. He tracked him down on Boston's Long Wharf at the British Coffee House. The two got into a melee. Robinson grabbed Otis's nose, and the two threw punches and whacked each other with their canes. Loyalists jostled Otis and called for his death while British offices stood by, watching. Ultimately, Otis was cudgeled on the head by Robinson and collapsed, dazed and bleeding. Months later, Otis still had a deep scar on his head that John Adams wrote "You could lay a finger in it."

Otis became a recluse. He began drinking heavily, wandering the taverns and streets, lamenting his opposition of the British. He was apparently suffering a mental break. He could not continue his work and was limited in his legal practice to brief periods of mental clarity. Wrote John Adams in January 1770, "He rambles like a ship without a helm . . .

Grave of James Otis Jr.

I fear, I tremble, I mourn for the man, and for his country." Later, in February 1771, Adams wrote that Otis was "raving mad, raving against father, wife, brother, sister, friend."

Otis was elected to the House again that year but was unable to contribute, propped up socially by John and Sam Adams. That December, Thomas Hutchinson, in a letter to Governor Bernard, said, "Otis was carried off today in a postchaise, bound hand and foot. He has been as good as his word—set the Province in a flame and perished in the attempt."

Otis was passed between family and friends as he battled mental illness, living in the countryside. After the Revolution in 1783, Governor John Hancock held a dinner in Otis's honor, but he could not handle the speeches and toasts, and had to leave, returning home to the countryside.

In his unsteady state, Otis burned most of his papers, leaving historians with only the published correspondence with others.

On May 23, 1783, while standing in the doorway of a friend's home, watching a thunderstorm, Otis was struck and killed by lightning. He was buried in the Granary Burying Ground in Boston.

It must be noted that Otis did not literally invent the phrase "Taxation without representation is tyranny" but rather formed an idea that John Adams later paraphrased.

Adams eulogized Otis "as extraordinary in death as in life. He has left a character that will never die while the memory of the American Revolution remains."

Robert Treat Paine
(1731 – 1814)

The Objection Maker

Buried at Granary Burying Ground,
Boston, Massachusetts.

———•◦•———

Declaration of Independence

Robert Treat Paine was a Massachusetts delegate to the Continental Congress, a prosecutor in Boston of the British troops involved in the Boston Massacre, and a signer of the Declaration of Independence.

———•◦•———

Paine was born on March 11, 1731, in Boston, the fourth of five children of Reverend Thomas Paine, pastor of the Congregational Church at Weymouth, Massachusetts, and Eunice Treat. Paine has an impressive family history. The Treats were prominent in the British colonies, and the Paines can trace a lineage back to the *Mayflower*. Reverend Thomas Paine left the full-time ministry in 1730, moved the family to Boston, and entered business as a merchant.

Robert grew up in Boston near the prestigious Boston Latin School, which he attended. He finished at the top of his class and entered Harvard College at the age of fourteen. Just as he was graduating in 1749, his father lost his fortune and moved to Nova Scotia, leaving Robert to make his own way.

In 1750 Robert took a position as a teacher in the town of Lunenberg, Massachusetts. He moved back to Boston in 1751 and went to sea as a merchant selling manufactured goods. He traveled to the southern colonies, mainly North Carolina, the Azores, and Spain. These endeavors

Robert Treat Paine

were not very successful, and as a result, Paine briefly tried whaling in Greenland. This also failed, and in 1755 he began to study law with his relative Judge Samuel Willard in Lancaster, Massachusetts. When Willard was appointed colonel for the Crown Point expedition during the French and Indian War, Robert tried for an officer's commission but failed and served as chaplain of the regiment. He was encamped at Lake George for three months at the end of 1755. He moved back to Boston in the fall of 1756 and resumed the study of law under Benjamin Prat, later chief justice in New York. In May 1757, he was admitted to the bar. His father died that same month, leaving Robert with many debts and family responsibilities. Instead of setting up a practice, he was forced to go from town to town looking for business, called "circuit riding." In 1758, Paine qualified for practicing before the Superior Court. He moved to Taunton in southern Massachusetts and advanced his legal career, rising to a justice of the peace and barrister.

In 1766, he began to court Sally Cobb, the daughter of a leading merchant in Taunton, and married her on March 15, 1770. The couple had eight children together.

Paine's dedication to the patriot cause began as early as 1766 when he spoke out against the Stamp Act. In 1768, he served as Taunton's delegate at the provincial convention held in Boston to discuss the landing of British troops in Boston. While he decried the measures that the British were using against the colonies, he still believed, at least at this point, that separation from England would not be necessary.

The atmosphere changed in March 1770 when a clash between some Bostonians harassing British troops stationed in the city led them to open fire on the crowd killing five men. Paine was selected to prosecute the troops who were charged with murder. Defending the soldiers was John Adams, thus pitting two of Massachusetts' most eminent attorneys and future signers of the Declaration of Independence against one another. For both sides, trying the case required a great deal of delicacy and diplomacy. Nine soldiers were on trial, including their captain, Thomas Preston. Paine expressed that the core issue was whether the British Parliament could legally quarter an army in a town without its consent.

Following one of the first trials in American history to last for several days, even the crowd seemed exhausted. Testimony after testimony had been used to show both sides of the "Massacre" story. If the troops were assaulted at all, it constituted a provocation for which the law reduces the offense to manslaughter. All nine men were found not guilty of murder, while two were found guilty of manslaughter.

The trial did much to enhance Paine's reputation and popularity. In 1773, based on his work at the trial, he was elected to the House of Representatives from Taunton. That same year, Sam Adams formed a Committee of Correspondence to discuss the colonists' grievances, and he asked Paine to serve on the panel. He continued to represent Taunton in Massachusetts' Provincial Congress in 1774 and 1775.

Also, in 1774 he was elected to attend the First Continental Congress. He served there from October 5 to October 26, 1774, and on December 5 was elected to serve in the Second Continental Congress. Paine was among the members who were hesitant to cut ties entirely with their mother country and hoped that the formation of the Second Continental Congress would show the British a united colonial front, thereby leading them to negotiate. Even after Lexington, Concord, and Bunker Hill, he hoped that peace could prevail, and in July 1775, he signed the Olive Branch Petition that was sent to King George III as a final attempt to

The crypt of Robert Treat Paine.

avoid war. The King's rejection proved to be a turning point for many colonists. Paine may not have been among the original supporters of a war with England, but after the Olive Branch Petition rejection, he acknowledged its inevitability.

Paine was a vocal and involved member of the Continental Congress, often to the chagrin of others. Benjamin Rush nicknamed him the "Objection Maker" because, according to Rush, he seldom proposed anything but opposed nearly every measure proposed by other people. The record shows that he served punctually and faithfully on many congressional committees and chaired the Committee on Ordnance. He pressed hard for the domestic manufacture of gunpowder, muskets, and artillery. After signing the Declaration of Independence, Paine returned to Massachusetts and remained involved in government at the state level. He represented Taunton in the Massachusetts House of Representatives. He served as its speaker in 1777, a member of the Executive Council in 1779, and a member of the committee that drafted the state constitution in 1780. He became Massachusetts' first attorney general, serving from 1777 to 1790. He prosecuted the treason trials following Shay's Rebellion.

In 1783 Paine was offered a place on the State Supreme Court bench but initially declined, preferring to remain attorney general. He eventually accepted his friend Governor John Hancock's offer of an associate justiceship in 1790 and served until 1804, when he retired due to his increasing deafness. He enjoyed a peaceful retirement and died in 1814. He is buried in the Granary Burying Ground in Boston, two short blocks from his birthplace. The plaque over the vault of his grave reads, "One of the signers of the Declaration of Independence."

Timothy Pickering
(1745 – 1829)

Radical Federalist

Buried at Broad Street Cemetery,
Salem, Massachusetts.

———•◦•———

**Military • Postmaster General • Secretary of War
Secretary of State**

Timothy Pickering was first a soldier and had events happened differently; his unit would have fired the "Shot Heard Round the World" months
before Lexington and Concord. Pickering rose in the Continental Army
and was appointed Quartermaster General, in charge of all supplies
and logistics. During the Washington Administration, Pickering was
Postmaster General, then Secretary of War, and then Secretary of State.
He was also a US Senator from Massachusetts and served in the US
House of Representatives.

———•◦•———

Pickering, born July 17, 1745, in Salem, Massachusetts, was one
of nine children of Deacon Timothy Pickering and his wife, Mary (née
Wingate) Pickering. Pickering's older brother, John, later became the
Speaker of the Massachusetts House of Representatives.

Pickering was educated in the local grammar school before studying
law at Harvard College, where he graduated in 1763 at age 18. A local
minister said of Pickering, "From his youth, his townsmen proclaim him
assuming, turbulent, & headstrong." Pickering applied his aggressiveness
to public service, where he worked with the Essex County Register of
Deeds, John Higginson.

Timothy Pickering

Pickering received his first military commission in January 1766 as a lieutenant in the Essex County Militia. That Spring, on April 8, Pickering married Rebecca White of Salem, and he received a Master of Arts degree from Harvard.

The Massachusetts Bar admitted Pickering in 1768, and in 1769, he was promoted to captain in the militia. Around this time, he published in the local *Essex Gazette* his ideas about drilling soldiers. In 1775, these articles were published as *An Easy Plan for a Militia* and became the drill book used by the Continental Army before the arrival of Baron von Steuben and his *Regulations for the Order and Discipline of the Troops of the United States*.

In 1774, Pickering succeeded Higginson as the Register of Deeds. He was then elected as Salem's representative to the Massachusetts General Court and served in the Essex County Court of Common Pleas as a justice.

On Sunday, February 26, 1775, two months before Lexington and Concord, British Army Lieutenant Colonel Alexander Leslie was sent from Boston to search North Salem for contraband. Leslie chose Sunday morning, assuming Pickering and his militia would be in church. Unknown to Leslie, a fast rider had noticed the British troop movement at Marblehead and galloped off to North Salem. There, he warned the minister, Reverend Thomas Barnard Jr. of North Church, who left his pulpit and met the British troops at the nearby North River Bridge. Reverend Barnard warned Leslie that the militia was at the ready and that he should peacefully withdraw from the area. In what became known as "Leslie's Retreat," the British commander heeded the warning and returned to Boston, avoiding what would likely have been the opening battle of the American Revolution, postponing the "Shot Heard Round the World" for two more months.

Somewhat ironically, upon hearing of the action at Lexington and Concord that April, Pickering and his militia marched to take part but arrived too late to have an impact, though they did block the British retreat from Concord. They then joined the Siege of Boston.

In December 1776, Pickering moved his militia to New York with General Washington. The Commander in Chief noticed Pickering's abilities and offered the role of Adjutant General of the Continental Army with the rank of colonel. Said Washington of Pickering, he was "a great Military genius, cultivated by an industrious attention to the Study of War, and as a Gentleman of liberal education, distinguished zeal and great method and activity in Business." Pickering was also made a member of the Board of War. In this role, Pickering oversaw at the Sterling Iron Works the forging and building of the great chain across the Hudson River below West Point that thwarted British naval attack for the duration of the war. He was also praised by Congress for his work in supplying the troops. In reward for this, Congress appointed Pickering Quartermaster General in August 1780 until 1784.

In 1783, after the Revolution, Pickering moved to Philadelphia and engaged in a trading operation with friend Samuel Hodgdon, a merchant. At this time, lands along the northern tier of Pennsylvania were still in dispute with Connecticut, and the Third Pennamite-Yankee

War was underway. Pickering was held hostage for nineteen days by Connecticut claimants after trying to mediate a settlement on behalf of the Pennsylvania State Assembly. Pickering purchased land in the region and then moved to the Wyoming Valley in 1786. He helped to form Luzerne County, holding a series of offices. As a representative from Luzerne County in 1787, Pickering participated in the Pennsylvania convention to ratify the US Constitution and, from 1789 to 1790, the creation of a new state constitution.

In November 1790, President Washington, via Secretary of War Henry Knox, asked Pickering to negotiate several treaties with the Native Americans. He led the negotiations with the Six Nations at Tioga and then at Newtown Point in July 1791. Washington then appointed Pickering Postmaster General of the United States in 1791, following the resignation of Charles Osgood. Pickering also continued in his role negotiating treaties and completed the Treaty of Canandaigua with the Iroquois Confederacy in 1794, which recognized the Confederacy's sovereignty over a sizable territory within New York State and offered payments, including an annual allowance, in exchange for a peace agreement and the right of passage through Iroquois Territory for U.S. citizens.

In 1795, President Washington appointed Pickering Secretary of War following Henry Knox's resignation amid scandal. Pickering oversaw General Anthony Wayne's negotiations for the Treaty of Greenville with the Wyandots and the completion of the new frigates, *United States*, *Constitution*, and *Constellation*. He was also elected a member of the American Philosophical Society.

In Europe, the French Revolution was underway, as was war between England and France. The Washington Administration, though officially neutral, was split on who to support, with Secretary of State Thomas Jefferson friendly to France and Alexander Hamilton favoring England. As President Washington bent to Hamilton and his Federalists, Thomas Jefferson resigned his post in December 1793. Edmund Randolph, Jefferson's second cousin, was appointed Secretary of State, and former Secretary of State John Jay began negotiations with England. Suspicious of Randolph's intentions as someone favorable to France, like his cousin, Pickering helped to expose Randolph's objections to Jay's efforts. He produced a slanted translation of French documents that had been intercepted by the British Navy and informed President Washington that they proved Randolph's traitorous behavior. As the only cabinet member opposed to the Jay Treaty, Randolph resigned on August 19, 1795, following its narrow passage in the Senate. On August 20, President Washington appointed the loyal Federalist Pickering to the post on an interim basis. He was later confirmed by the Senate on December 10.

During his tenure as Secretary of State, Pickering maintained a pro-England posture, believing obligations to Revolutionary France were negated when the monarchy was overthrown. He also supported the Alien and Sedition Acts, permitting the arrest and deportation of non-citizens and clamping down on dissent in the press. During these years, a Quasi-War with France smoldered, with the French threatening American ships that were trading with England. Against Pickering's objections, President Adams sent a delegation, including Charles Cotesworth Pinckney, Elbridge Gerry, and John Marshall, to France to negotiate a peace, but when the French attempted to bribe them, outrage ensued in what became known as the XYZ Affair. Following the publication of the related papers to the affair, Pickering endorsed open war with France.

In 1799, Pickering sailed to England on the merchant ship *Washington*. On October 24, the French privateer *Bellona* attacked *Washington*, but the Americans repelled the attack despite inferior guns and crew.

Ultimately, President Adams desired peace with France, to which Pickering and Alexander Hamilton were opposed. Adams asked for Pickering's resignation, but he refused. Adams then dismissed Pickering on May 12, 1800.

John Adams failed to win a second term, yielding to Thomas Jefferson as the new President of the United States. In 1802, Pickering led a Federalist New England secessionist movement that sought to join the New England states with Pennsylvania and Virginia and make him president. Pickering sought to be "exempt from the corrupt and corrupting influence and oppression of the aristocratic democrats of the South." Failing that, Pickering was named to the US Senate from Massachusetts in 1803, serving until 1811. He opposed the Louisiana Purchase of 1803 and the annexation of Spanish West Florida in 1810 as unconstitutional, fearing they would increase the South's power.

In 1807, Pickering opposed President Jefferson's Embargo Act, which sought to restrict foreign trade during the Napoleonic Wars. He conferenced with British envoy George Rose, persuading British Foreign Secretary George Canning to maintain a hard line against America, hoping that Jefferson would act more severely and, therefore, weaken the Democratic-Republicans.

When Pickering published harsh criticism of the Embargo Act, he was charged with reading confidential documents in an open Senate session before an injunction of secrecy was removed. For this, the Senate censured Pickering on January 2, 1811, 20 to 7. He was the first US Senator to be censured. He lost his reelection bid and returned to his farm in Salem for a year.

In 1812, Pickering was elected to the US House of Representatives, serving for two terms until 1817. During this time, he renewed his call for Northern secession as part of the Essex Junto at the Hartford Convention in 1814. The remaining Federalists were unhappy with the concentration of power in the South and the Madison Administration's prosecution of the War of 1812.

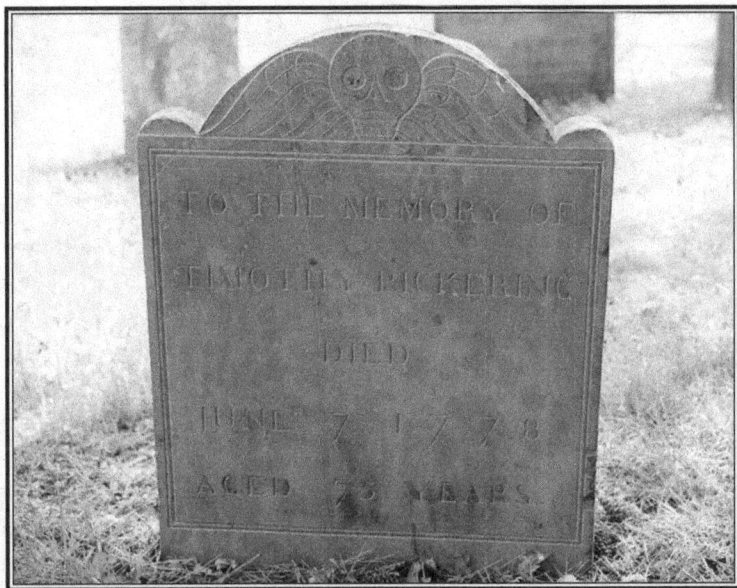

Grave of Timothy Pickering

During his time in Congress, Pickering was elected a Fellow of the American Academy of Arts and Sciences in 1815. However, he lost his re-election bid in 1816 and retired from politics to his farm in Salem.

Pickering died on his farm on January 29, 1829, at age 83. He was buried at the Broad Street Cemetery in Salem.

Fort Pickering, in Salem, Massachusetts, was named for him, as was the World War II Liberty ship SS *Timothy Pickering*, lost off Sicily in 1943. The Pickering home in Salem remained in the family until the 1990s.

Paul Revere
(1735 – 1818)

"Listen, my children, and you shall hear . . ."

Buried at Granary Burying Ground,
Boston, Massachusetts.

Militia Officer • Courier • Industrialist

Paul Revere was quite a guy—smart, talented, brave, dependable, creative, and industrious. He was known and respected in the Boston area but was transformed into a national folk hero by Henry Wadsworth Longfellow's poem "Paul Revere's Ride." His life was long and productive, involving industry, politics and community service. He played a number of important roles in the American Revolution.

Paul Revere was born in North End Boston on or about January 1, 1735. His father, Apollos Rivoire, was a French Huguenot immigrant who changed his name after arriving in America. He was a goldsmith. He married Deborah Hitchborn in 1729, and the couple had twelve children, of which Paul was the third.

He attended the North Boston Writing School between the ages of seven and thirteen after which he became an apprentice to his father. His father died in 1754 when Paul was nineteen, leaving him to support his mother and siblings. Two years later, in 1756, Revere was commissioned as a second lieutenant in the Massachusetts Artillery and sent to fight the French in upstate New York. He only served a short while, and when he returned in November 1756, he began in earnest to build the

Paul Revere

family silver business. He returned with neither laurels nor war stories that would entertain.

In August 1757, Revere married Sarah Orne. The couple had eight children. Soon after Sarah died in 1773, Revere married Rachel Walker, with whom he also had eight children.

Revere's primary vocation was as a silversmith. His shop produced pieces from simple spoons to magnificent tea sets. His work was well regarded during his lifetime and is highly prized today. He supplemented his income by working as a copperplate engraver. He also tried his hand at dentistry, opening his own office in Boston in 1768. Being a skilled craftsman, he was good at making artificial teeth. One of his customers, who became a good friend, was Joseph Warren, a prominent doctor and a major general in the Continental Army.

In the years leading up to the Battles of Lexington and Concord Revere worked tirelessly for the patriot cause. He was a member of the Freemasons, the Mechanics Union, the Sons of Liberty and other groups. He became a nexus in the social networks of the Revolution. He gathered intelligence by watching the movements of British soldiers and was a courier for the Boston Committee of Correspondence and the Massachusetts Committee of Safety, riding express to the Continental Congress in Philadelphia.

In November 1773, the merchant ship *Dartmouth* arrived in Boston carrying the first shipment of tea made under the terms of the Tea Act, which authorized the British East India Company to ship tea bypassing colonial merchants. Revere and Joseph Warren organized a watch over the ship so that it would not be unloaded. Revere took his turn at guard duty. He was a ringleader when, on December 13, 1773, he and fifty other patriots boarded the ships in the harbor and dumped the tea.

His activism extended beyond Boston when he began work as a courier and rode from Boston to New York and to Philadelphia to spread information about activities in the colonies. After the British seized a supply of the colony's gunpowder, he organized a system to detect and warn others of British troop movements. He once rode fifty miles to Portsmouth, New Hampshire, to warn the locals there of an impending seizure.

When Joseph Warren and his associates learned the British were moving troops out of Boston and planned to arrest Sam Adams and John Hancock in Lexington, Revere was sent to warn them and locals in Concord where weapons and supplies were being stored. At about 10 PM on April 18, 1775, Revere set out on horseback. A soldier named William Dawes had been sent about an hour earlier on a different route with the same objective. Revere arrived first, and Dawes about half an hour later. Adams and Hancock, being warned, were able to avoid arrest. As Revere and Dawes set out to warn Concord, they were joined by Dr. Samuel Prescott, who was on his way home in Concord. Ironically Prescott was the only one to make it. A British mounted patrol intercepted the three riders. They captured Revere, but Dawes and Prescott escaped. Dawes, however, was thrown from his horse as he fled and made his way back to Lexington. Prescott made it to Concord after riding through woods and swamps. The Battles of Lexington and Concord would spark the Revolutionary War the next day. The first shot fired in Lexington

A romantic depiction of Paul Revere's nighttime ride to warn of the approaching British.

became known as "the shot heard round the world." The ride has been commemorated most notably by Henry Wadsworth Longfellow's 1861 poem, "Paul Revere's Ride," which shaped popular memory of the event despite its factual inaccuracies. The famous opening verse began:

> LISTEN, my children, and you shall hear
> Of the midnight ride of Paul Revere,
> On the eighteenth of April, in seventy-five;
> Hardly a man is now alive
> Who remembers that famous day and year.

After Lexington and Concord, Revere felt it unsafe to return to Boston and boarded in Watertown, Massachusetts. He was denied a commission in the newly formed Continental Army. He found other ways to help, however, such as manufacturing gunpowder. Gunpowder was in short supply, and Revere managed to build a gunpowder mill in present-day Canton, Massachusetts. The mill produced tons of gunpowder for the Patriot cause. Tragically, he was also called to do some dental work. His friend General Joseph Warren was killed at the Battle of

Bunker Hill on June 17, 1775. Nine months later, in early 1776, Revere was called upon to help identify his friend. Months had passed since the battle, but Revere recognized the artificial teeth and dental prosthetic he had implanted.

He returned to Boston in 1776 and was commissioned a major of infantry in the Massachusetts Militia and, in May, transferred to Artillery. In November, he was promoted to Lt. Colonel and stationed at Castle William, defending Boston Harbor. In the summer of 1779, he was appointed commander of the field artillery in a large expedition to dislodge the British from a new base they had established on Penobscot Bay. Forty-five American ships sailed into Penobscot Bay, and the British

Revere's tomb marker

were grossly outnumbered; the Americans did not attack. Land and sea commanders squabbled over control and could not agree on strategy or tactics. The arrival of British reinforcements led to the destruction of the entire Massachusetts fleet. An orderly retreat up the Penobscot River turned into a panicked rout. The American land forces became scattered, and most made their way back to Boston on foot. A variety of charges were made against Revere. In September 1779, a Board of

Paul Revere's monument

Inquiry held hearings on the matter, and the results were inconclusive, but he was asked to resign his post. The Board did find Commodore Dudley Saltonstall, the commander of the expedition, to be primarily responsible and he was dismissed from the Navy for ineptitude. Revere was unhappy with this outcome and determined to receive a proper hearing; he petitioned the Massachusetts government seven times for a court-martial before one was finally convened in February 1782. The court, consisting of one general and twelve captains ruled that Revere be found not guilty of all charges. He accepted the result as a vindication of his honor. While his conduct as a military officer was perhaps less than exemplary, the circumstances were unusual, and neither he nor his forces were professional military men.

Revere lived for almost forty years after the war, becoming renowned as a craftsman. Pioneering in a number of areas, he designed and printed the first issue of Continental paper currency, cast cannons and bells in bronze and built the first copper-rolling mill in America. One of his largest bells still rings in Boston's Kings Chapel. He provided copper sheeting for the dome of the State House and the hull of the USS *Constitution* when it was re-coppered in 1803.

Paul Revere died on May 10, 1818, at the age of 83, at his home on Charter Street in Boston. He is buried in the Granary Burying Ground on Tremont Street.

Artemas Ward
(1727 – 1800)

First Commander-in-Chief

Buried at Mountain View Cemetery,
Shrewsbury Center, Massachusetts.

Major General • Colonial Governor • Continental Congress
United States House of Representatives

Artemas Ward was a member of a noteworthy New England family who served as a colonel in the Massachusetts Militia during the French and Indian War. Following Lexington and Concord, he answered the patriot call and was initially the first commander-in-chief of colonial forces. During the Siege of Boston in 1775, prior to Washington's arrival, Ward was the commanding officer of the patriot forces there, coordinating the arrival and positioning of cannon and the defense of Bunker and Breed's Hills. While he commanded from his headquarters, he was the planner of the defense that proved tenacious for the advancing Redcoats. He was then appointed one of the four major generals subordinate to George Washington. After the British left Boston, Ward returned to civilian life and was active politically, ultimately serving in the Continental Congress and then the Second and Third Congresses in the House of Representatives. In his writings about the American Revolution, President John Adams eulogized Ward as: "universally esteemed, beloved and confided in by his army and his country."

Artemas Ward, the son of Colonel Nahum Ward and his wife Martha (née How or Howe) Ward, the sixth of seven children, was born on

Artemas Ward

November 26, 1727, in Shrewsbury, Massachusetts. The elder Ward was deeply involved in the community and was credited as one of the founders of Shrewsbury. He was a lawyer who served in several political offices, including selectman, representative in the General Court, Justice of the Peace for Worcester County, and Judge of the Court of Common Pleas as well. He was also a land developer, farmer, merchant, and sea captain. Martha's father had also been a sea captain. The Ward family was one of the first to settle on Massachusetts Bay, descended from William Ward, a Puritan, who arrived in Sudbury and then Marlborough.

Young Artemas attended the local common schools, sharing a private tutor with his siblings. He graduated from Harvard in 1748 with a bachelor's degree. He followed this with a master's degree in 1751 and taught for a while at Harvard. While in graduate school, on July 31, 1750, Ward married Sarah Trowbridge (1724–1788), a daughter of Reverend

Caleb Trowbridge and Hannah Walter of Groton, Massachusetts. The Trowbridges were descendants of Cotton and Increase Mather. The young couple soon returned to Shrewsbury, where Ward opened a general store. Over the next fourteen years, the couple had eight children: Ithamar (1752), Nahum (1754), Sara (1756), Thomas (1758), Artemas Jr. (1762), Henry Dana (1768), Martha (1760), and Maria (1764).

Ward continued to study law after Harvard and became involved in the community politically. His first office was as a township assessor for Worcester County in 1751. Next, in 1752, at only age 25, he was elected as a justice of the peace and to the Massachusetts Provincial Assembly, also known as the "General Court," serving many terms in that body.

During the French and Indian War, between 1755 and 1757, Ward alternated between military and political duties. In 1755, Major Ward was in the 3rd Regiment of soldiers drawn from Worcester County, garrisoning the western frontier of the colony. In 1757, he was promoted to colonel of the regiment, which now included Middlesex and Worcester Counties.

Following the war, in 1762, Ward was named a justice on the Court of Common Pleas, rising to Chief Justice over the next thirteen years. During the Stamp Act crisis, Ward was very vocal in the General Court, speaking out second only to James Otis. He was on the taxation committee with Sam Adams and John Hancock. Given his protesting nature, in 1767, Royal Governor Francis Bernard revoked Ward's military commission. The following year, the governor voided Ward's election to the General Court, but Ward would not be silenced. Soon, he was back among the Governor's Council under Thomas Hutchinson, especially at the time of the Boston Tea Party in 1773.

Following the Boston Port Act, Parliament's response to the Boston Tea Party, on October 3, 1774, the 3rd Regiment of Massachusetts Militia resigned en masse from British service. They unanimously elected Ward as their leader and marched to Shrewsbury to inform him. Governor Hutchinson then abolished the assembly, but patriots established Committees of Safety across the colony. The new Provincial Congress then, on October 27, 1774, appointed Ward as General and Commander-in-Chief of all Massachusetts Militia.

As the Second Continental Congress met in early 1775, following Lexington and Concord, they appointed Artemas Ward as

Commander-in-Chief of all colonial forces. Ward had been ill at home and missed the initial battle but quickly rallied in his new role to organize the forces to counter the British occupation of Boston. It was Ward who drilled the various militia groups who arrived to resist the Crown's invaders. It was Ward, who planned the defenses, including the movement of cannon and men to Bunker and Breed's Hills. It was Ward who assigned Israel Putnam to these defenses. While the battle on June 17, 1775, was a loss for the rebels, it cost the British dearly, sending the message that any suppression of the Americans was going to be difficult.

On June 19, as the Continental Congress met in Philadelphia, they selected George Washington of Virginia to be the Commander-in-Chief for all Continental forces and sent him to Boston to take over from Ward, who remained in command until July 2, 1775. Ward was retained, with Charles Lee, Philip Schuyler, and Israel Putnam as major generals under Washington. Horatio Gates was named adjutant-general. Over the intervening months, Washington held the British in check, besieging the British in Boston. In November, he sent Henry Knox to retrieve the captured cannon from Fort Ticonderoga and reposition them on the Dorchester Heights above Boston. The cannons were in place by January 1776, under Ward's command. Soon after, the British ended their occupation of Boston on March 17, 1776.

As the British left Boston, Washington soon followed them to New York. Ward remained behind, in command of the forces around Boston, until March 1777, when he resigned from the army citing ill health.

Almost immediately after the British left the area, while still in command of the local military forces, Ward returned as Chief Justice of the Court of Common Please for Worcester County. In 1777, after resigning from the military, he was named a member of the Massachusetts Executive Council until 1779, serving as its President, making him the colony's governor until the new Massachusetts constitution was adopted in 1780. He was also elected to the state House of Representatives, serving until 1785, rising to Speaker in his final year.

When Continental Congressman Timothy Edwards resigned on June 2, 1779, the Massachusetts legislature selected Ward as his replacement. However, Ward did not take his seat until the following year. Ward served in the Continental Congress, now back in Philadelphia, from January

Grave marker of Artemas Ward

1780 until May 1782. During this time, the Articles of Confederation were adopted.

Ward returned to Massachusetts and continued his role in the legislature. As Speaker of the House and Justice of the Peace of the Worcester Court in 1786, he was involved in suppressing Shays Rebellion, facing down the rebels at his courthouse steps.

Following the signing of the U.S. Constitution in September 1787, Ward remained in Massachusetts in the courts. But in November 1790, he ran for and won a seat in the Second and then the Third U.S. Congresses, serving in the House of Representatives from 1791 until 1795. Ward was one of only nine representatives to vote against the Eleventh Amendment to the Constitution concerning states' rights and the judiciary.

Ward returned home to Shrewsbury in March 1795. In December 1797, he retired from his judicial duties. He died at his home on October 28, 1800, at the age of 72. He was laid to rest at Mountain View Cemetery in Shrewsbury.

Ward has been remembered in a number of ways. In 1778, the town of Ward was named after him. However, in 1837, following complaints to the postal services, the town's name was changed to Auburn because Ward was too similar to nearby Ware, Massachusetts.

The Artemas Ward House, the original home of Nahum Ward, remains as a museum at 786 Main Street, Shrewsbury, Massachusetts.

In Washington, D.C., on the campus of American University, Ward Circle is at the convergence of Massachusetts and Nebraska Avenues. In 1938, a ten-foot marble statue of Ward was erected in this circle, modeled after a painting by Charles Wilson Peale. At its base is inscribed "Artemas Ward, 1727-1800, Son of Massachusetts, Graduate of Harvard College, Judge and Legislator, Delegate 1780-1781 Continental Congress, Soldier in Three Wars, First Commander of the Patriotic Forces." American University has since named the home of its School of Public Affairs the Ward Circle Building in honor of Artemas Ward.

Joseph Warren
(1741 – 1775)

Hero of Bunker Hill

Buried at Forest Hills Cemetery,
Jamaica Plain, Massachusetts.

Military

Joseph Warren was a physician and Major General who was a key leader for liberty in Massachusetts at the outset of the American Revolution. He barely escaped death at Lexington and Concord and was subsequently martyred at the Battle of Bunker Hill where he fought as a private beside his men in the trench atop Breed's Hill rather than take overall command from the more experienced General Israel Putnam.

Joseph Warren was born June 11, 1741, in Roxbury, Massachusetts. He was the son of Joseph Warren, a farmer, and Mary (nee Stevens) Warren. The elder Warren fell from a ladder in their orchard and died when Joseph was only 14. Young Joseph attended the Roxbury Latin School and enrolled at Harvard College where he graduated in 1759 at the age of 18. He taught for a year and studied medicine. In September of 1764, he married an 18-year-old heiress Elizabeth Hooten. The two had four children: Elizabeth, Joseph, Mary, and Richard.

Joseph practiced medicine and surgery in Boston and was an avid Mason. Through his wife's connections, he had an interesting list of patients including John Adams and his family. Warren once saved 7-year-old John Quincy Adams' finger from amputation. He also had Loyalist patients such as the children of Thomas Hutchinson and General Thomas

Portrait of Joseph Warren by John Singleton Copley, 1765.

Gage and his wife Margaret. It is the latter to whom some suggest he had an affair that gave him inside information about British military movements, but this is disputed.

Warren was also a leader of the patriot cause, writing an incendiary essay in the newspaper in 1768 under the pseudonym A True Patriot. His publishers were put on trial, but no jury would indict them.

Warren became Master of the Lodge in 1769 at the time Paul Revere was its Secretary. At this time, he also became involved in the Sons of Liberty, associating with John Hancock, Samuel Adams, and others. In February 1770, he performed an autopsy on the body of 12-year-old Christopher Seider who had been killed in Boston in a protest. The reaction to his funeral led to an uprising resulting in the Boston Massacre.

Following Elizabeth's death in 1772 at only 26, Joseph was a widower with young children. This did not dissuade him from his convictions. He authored a song "Free America" which was set to the melody of "The

British Grenadiers." It was published in many colonial newspapers in 1774. As tensions rose around Boston, Warren was appointed to the Boston Committee of Correspondence. He spoke publicly at commemorations of the Boston Massacre, the last time in March 1775 while the city was occupied by the British. Warren drafted the Suffolk Resolves, endorsed by the Continental Congress, in resistance to the Coercive Acts. Following this, he was appointed President of the Massachusetts Provincial Congress—the highest position in the colony. Around this time he became engaged to Mercy Scollay.

On April 18, 1775, Warren got wind that the British were about to march on Concord, through Lexington, to capture the munitions stored there by the colonials. Warren sent William Dawes and Paul Revere on their rides that evening to warn Hancock and Adams in Lexington. The next morning, he left Boston and helped coordinate the militia alongside William Heath as the British returned to Boston. Warren was shot by a musket, the ball striking his wig without consequence.

When his mother learned of his brush with death, she begged him not to risk his life any further. Warren responded, "Where danger is, dear mother, there must your son be. Now is no time for any of America's children to shrink from any hazard. I will set her free or die." Warren continued to recruit and organize the militia while negotiating with General Gage as the leader of the Provincial Congress.

As the British continued to prepare to engage the colonials, Warren was commissioned as a major general by the Provincial Congress on June 14, 1775. A few days later, in the moments before the Battle of Bunker Hill, Warren arrived on the field as the militia was forming and asked where the heaviest fighting was likely to be. General Israel Putnam pointed to Breed's Hill. Warren then volunteered to join the fight as a private, leaving command with Putnam and Colonel William Prescott, who implored him not to do so. Both wished to serve him as their commander. Warren declined believing the two were more experienced as soldiers.

Warren joined the men in the trench atop Breed's Hill and helped hold the ranks against attacks from superior numbers. He declared to the British, "These fellows say we won't fight! By Heaven, I hope I shall die up

Bronze statue of Joseph Warren at Forest Hills
Cemetery in Jamaica Plain, Massachusetts (photo by
Lawrence Knorr).

to my knees in blood!" Warren continued to fight until out of ammunition. He remained to allow his militia to escape as the British made their
third and final assault. Warren was killed instantly by a musket ball to
the head, likely fired by Lieutenant Lord Rawdon who recognized him.
His body was stripped and he was bayoneted repeatedly until unrecog-
nizable. He was then shoved into a shallow ditch with another soldier.
"I stuffed the scoundrel with another rebel into one hole, and there he
is and his seditious principles may remain," said Captain Walter Laurie.

Said General Thomas Gage, the death of Warren was "worth the death
of 500 men." In a letter to John Adams, Benjamin Hichborn described
further damage inflicted on Warren's body two days after the battle by a
Brit: "In a day or two after, Drew went upon the Hill again opened the
dirt that was thrown over Doctor Warren, spit in his Face, jumped on his

stomach, and at last cut off his head and committed every act of violence upon his body."

The next day his friend James Warren (no relation) wrote a letter to his wife, Mercy Otis Warren,

> . . . The British are reinforced but have not advanced, so things remain at present as they were we have killed many men & have killed & wounded about [six] hundred by the best accounts I can get. Among the first of which to our inexpressible grief is my friend Doctor Warren who was killed. it is supposed in the lines on the hill at Charlestown in a manner more glorious to himself than the fate of Wolf on the plains of Abraham. Many other officers are wounded and some killed. it is Impossible to describe the confusion in this place, women & children flying into the country, armed men going to the field, and wounded men returning from there fill the Streets.

Loyalist Peter Oliver wrote in 1782 that had Warren lived, George Washington would have been an obscurity. Military historian Ethan

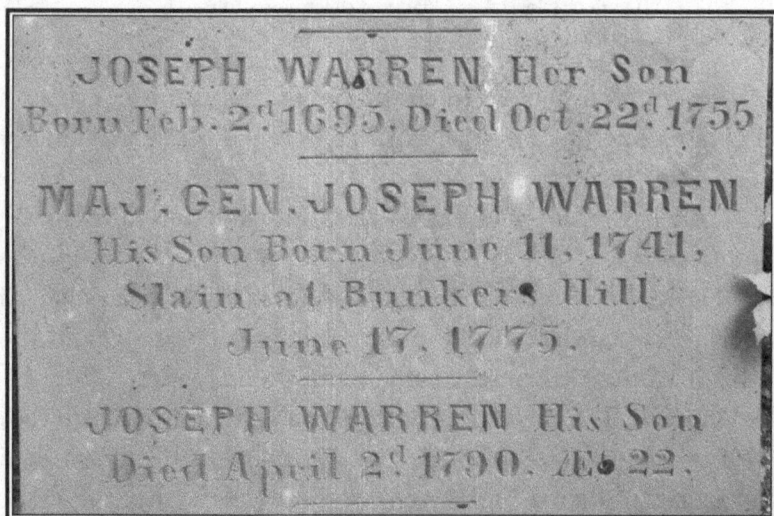

Marker for Joseph Warren at Forest Hills Cemetery in Jamaica Plain, Massachusetts (photo by Lawrence Knorr).

Rafuse wrote, "No man, with the possible exception of Samuel Adams, did so much to bring about the rise of a movement powerful enough to lead the people of Massachusetts to revolution."

Ten months after his death, his brothers and Paul Revere dug up and identified Warren's remains thanks to an artificial tooth Revere had placed in the jaw. Warren was buried at the Granary Burying Ground in Boston. Later, in 1825, he was moved to St. Paul's Church before being placed in the family's vault at Forest Hills Cemetery in 1855, where he remains. Mercy Scollay continued to care for the Warren children and received assistance from John Hancock, Samuel Adams, Mercy Otis Warren, Benedict Arnold, and the Continental Congress. John Warren, Joseph's youngest brother, was a surgeon at Bunker Hill and for the rest of the war. He later founded Harvard Medical School and co-founded the Massachusetts Medical Society.

Warren is honored by at least four statues—three in Boston and one in Warren, Pennsylvania. Numerous towns, counties, and streets are named after him. Several ships have borne his name.

Mercy Otis Warren
(1728 – 1814)

The Muse of the Revolution

Buried at Burial Hill,
Plymouth, Massachusetts.

———•✦•———

Poet • Political Playwright • Thought Leader

This founder was undoubtedly ahead of her time. When Benjamin Franklin was writing in *Poor Richard's Almanac,* "Girls, Mark my words and know, For men of sense/ Your strongest charms are native innocence," she was busy with her education, refining her talents and losing that aforementioned innocence. In 1848 she was hailed by Elizabeth Elett as "perhaps the most remarkable woman who lived at the time of the Revolution." Her writings were admired by her friend John Adams whom she would come to call a monarchist. She also argued in print against the ratification of the Constitution unless it contained a Bill of Rights. Her biographer, Nancy Rubin Stuart, referred to her as "The Muse of the Revolution." One hundred seventy-three years after her death, she became the first woman to have her portrait unveiled in Boston's historic Faneuil Hall. This remarkable woman's name was Mercy Otis Warren.

———•✦•———

Warren was born on September 14, 1728, in West Barnstable, Massachusetts. She was the third of thirteen children and the first daughter produced by Colonel James Otis and Mary Allyne Otis. Just six of her siblings lived to adulthood. Her father was an attorney who

Mercy Otis Warren

served as a judge for the Barnstable Court of Common Pleas. He was also active in local politics and was elected to the Massachusetts House of Representatives in 1745. It was during this time that Warren's father also became a colonel of the local militia.

In these colonial times, it was unusual, even for well-born girls like Warren, to receive the education afforded to young men. Instead, girls were expected to learn various household duties and assist in keeping up the homestead. Warren found some escape from her chores in books brought into the house by her older brothers, who were being tutored by James Otis's brother-in-law, the Reverend John Russell. Warren pleaded with her father to join her brothers in their studies, and no one knows why he eventually agreed. One popular theory is that when her brother Joseph decided to end his educational pursuits, Warren's father permitted her to take his place with the Reverend Russell.

The Reverend was widely recognized as one of the best-educated men in the local area. Under his tutelage, Warren studied the works of Milton and Shakespeare and learned to write. Her later work would reflect the style and cadence used by Reverend Russell in his sermons. She also studied British history reading, according to her biographer, Raleigh's *History of the World*.

There is no doubt that Warren's growing up in the Otis household also influenced her evolving political views. Her father was a well-known critic of British rule, and he often found himself at odds with the colonial governor Thomas Hutchinson. She and her siblings have been described as raised "in the midst of revolutionary ideals."

On November 14, 1754, at the age of 26, Warren married James Warren. The letters exchanged between the couple over the years illustrate the respect and bond the two felt for each other. In one letter, James wrote, "I have read one Excellent sermon this day and heard two others. What next can I do better but to write to a Saint." Warren's letter in response stated, "Your spirit I admire were a few thousands on the Continent of a similar disposition we might defy the power of Britain." Through the course of their marriage, the couple would produce five sons.

James Warren shared many of his wife's revolutionary views. He also had a successful political career. In 1765 he was elected to the Massachusetts House of Representatives. He would serve as the speaker of this body and as the President of the Massachusetts Provincial Congress. During the Revolutionary War, he also served for a time as paymaster to Washington's army. It was during his political career that he struck up a friendship with John Adams. In 1767 Adams enjoyed a Sunday dinner with the Warrens. Afterward, he wrote to his wife Abigail, "In Coll. Warren and his lady, I find friends." Despite the age differences between the couples, the Warrens were more than a decade older. By 1772 drawn together by their shared views, they were good friends.

In December of 1773, Adams wrote to James Warren relative to the Boston Tea Party. The letter included a request. "Make my compliments to Mrs. Warren and tell her I want a poetical genius to describe a late frolic among the sea nymphs and goddesses. I wish to see a late glorious event, celebrated by a certain poetic pen, which has no equal . . . in this country." The result was Warren's composition titled "The Squabble of the Sea Nymphs or the Sacrifice of the Tuscararoes." Though Warren harbored doubts about the merits of her composition Adams not only arranged for its publication in the *Boston Gazette*, he sent Mr. Warren another letter where he described the poem as "one of the incontestable evidences of real genius."

Warren was more than a poet. She was also a playwright and a historian. Her play *The Adulateur* was published in 1773. It was directed against her father's adversary Massachusetts Governor Thomas Hutchinson. The play predicted the Revolutionary War. Hutchinson is represented by the character Rapatio. The fact that this character represented Hutchinson was so thinly veiled that Massachusetts citizens who identified with the patriot cause began referring to him by that name.

The same year that *The Adulateur* was published, Rapatio made another appearance in a play Warren penned titled *The Defeat*. In the biography, *The Muse of the Revolution*, Stuart describes this work as "one of the Revolutionary era's most scorching indictments of the British abuse of colonial liberties." The play contributed to increased resistance to Hutchinson's rule and is believed to have played a significant role in the British decision to replace him in office. Also, these works have been credited to have influenced many colonists to join the patriot cause.

In 1774 Warren sent her husband the first two acts of her latest play titled *The Group*. This satire focused on what would happen if the British monarch eliminated the Massachusetts charter of rights. The play had a second theme, namely championing the rights of married women. Warren cautioned her husband that whatever he did with the piece to make sure that the author's identity was not revealed. She knew that the English authorities would view the piece as treasonous. James Warren sent the work to John Adams in Philadelphia, and Adams immediately had the play published. Soon it was circulated in both Boston and New York and was warmly received by those sympathetic to the patriot cause. John Adams praised the work and writing the author's husband described her as "an incomparable satirist."

Warren herself regularly corresponded with a group of friends that included Abigail Adams, Martha Washington, and the renowned English historian Catherine Macaulay. According to the author Katherine Anthony in her work *First Lady of the Revolution: The Life of Mercy Otis*

Warren Macaulay had "a more profound influence on Warren than any other woman of her era."

When the American Revolution began, Warren began recording the events of the day. These writings would form the foundation for her *History of the Rise, Progress, and Termination of the American Revolution*, published in 1805. This was one of the first nonfiction books written by a woman in the United States. The history was admired by then President

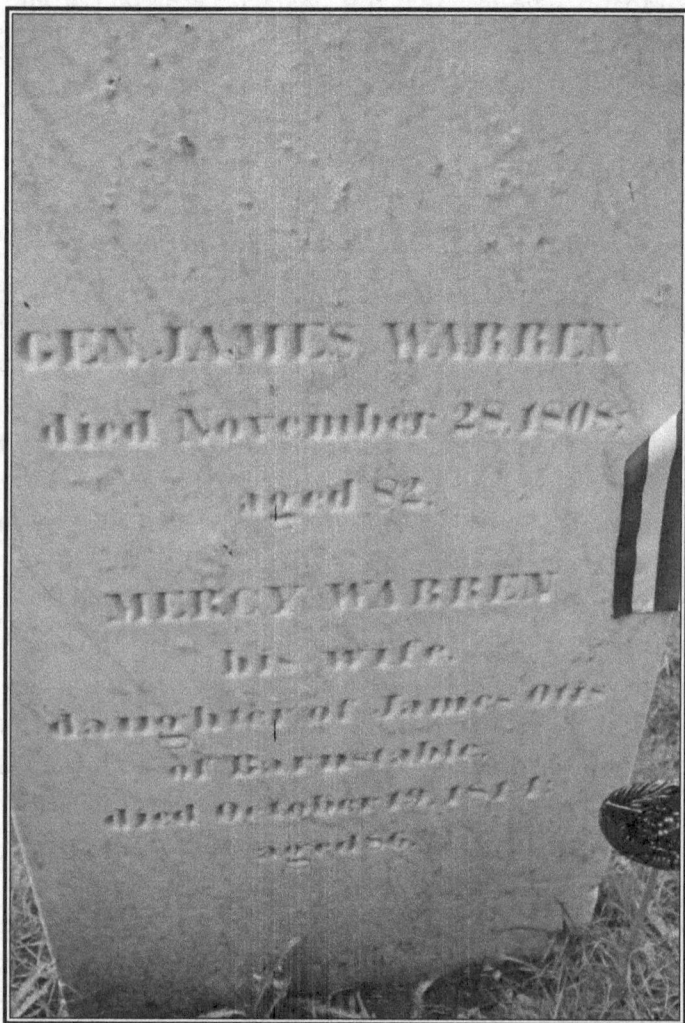

Mercy Otis Warren marker.

Thomas Jefferson, who ordered copies for himself and his cabinet members. John Adams failed to share Jefferson's enthusiasm. The sharp and critical comments on the Adams presidency resulted in damaging their friendship. Among her criticisms was her view that Adams had "forgotten the principles of the American Revolution." Adams remarked that "History is not the province of the ladies." The two continued to argue via letter until they reconciled their differences in 1812.

Before publishing her history in 1790, Warren released the first work bearing her name *Poems, Dramatic and Miscellaneous*. This book was made up of political poems and two plays. Two years earlier, she had written *Observations on the New Constitution*. This piece was critical of the proposed Constitution for failing to include specific provisions for freedom of speech and the freedom of the press. Eventually, ten of Warren's objections would appear in the Bill of Rights. For years Observations was thought to be the work of Elbridge Gerry until one of her descendants found a reference to the piece in a letter sent in 1787 to Catherine Macaulay, which resulted in recognition of Warren as the author.

Warren died at the age of 86 on October 19, 1814. She was laid to rest at Burial Hill in Plymouth, Massachusetts. Alexander Hamilton had Warren in mind when he stated, "In the career of dramatic composition at least, female genius in the United States has outstripped the male."

Sources

Books, Magazines, Journals, Files:

Alexander, Edward P. *Revolutionary Conservative: James Duane of New York*. New York: Ams Press, 1978.

Anthony, Katharine Susan. *First Lady of the Revolution; The Life of Mercy Otis Warren*. Port Washington, N.Y.: Kennikat Press, 1972.

Appleby, Joyce. *Inheriting the Revolution: The First Generation of Americans*. Cambridge, Massachusetts: Harvard University Press, 2000.

Atkinson, Rick. *The British Are Coming: The War for America, Lexington to Princeton, 1775-1777*. New York: Henry Holt & Co. 2019.

Bordewich, Fergus M. *The First Congress: How James Madison, George Washington, and a Group of Extraordinary Men Invented the Government*. New York: Simon and Schuster Paperbacks, 2016.

Boudreau, George W. *Independence: A Guide to Historic Philadelphia*. Yardley, Pennsylvania: Westholme Publishing, LLC. 2012.

Bowen, Catherine Drinker. *Miracle at Philadelphia: The Story of the Constitutional Convention May to September 1787*. Boston, Massachusetts: Little, Brown & Company, 1966.

Breen, T.H, *George Washington's Journey: The President Forges a New Nation*. New York: Simon & Schuster. 2016.

Brookhiser, Richard. *Gentleman Revolutionary: Gouverneur Morris The Rake Who Wrote the Constitution*. New York: Free Press, 2003.

———. *John Marshall: The Man Who Made the Supreme Court*. New York: Basic Books. 2018.

Brush, Edward Hale. *Rufus King and His Times*. New York: N.L. Brown, 1926.

Chadwick, Bruce. I Am Murdered: *George Wythe, Thomas Jefferson, and the Killing That Shocked a New Nation*. Hoboken, New Jersey: John Wiley & Sons, 2009.

Chambers, II, John Whiteclay. *The Oxford Companion to American Military History*. Oxford: Oxford University Press, 1999.

Commager, Henry Steele & Richard B. Morris. *The Spirit of 'Seventy-Six: The Story of the American Revolution as Told by Participants*. New York: Harper & Rowe, 1967.

Cole, Ryan. *Light-Horse Harry Lee: The Rise and Fall of a Revolutionary Hero*. Washington, D.C.: Regnery History. 2019.

Conlin, Joseph R. *The Morrow Book of Quotations in American History*. New York: William Morrow and Company, Inc., 1984.

Daniels, Jonathan. *Ordeal of Ambition*. Garden City, New York: Doubleday & Company, Inc., 1970.

Dann, John C. *The Revolution Remembered: Eyewitness Accounts of the War for Independence*. Chicago: University of Chicago Press, 1980.

SOURCES

DeRose, Chris. *Founding Rivals: Madison vs. Monroe: The Bill of Rights and the Election that Saved a Nation*. New York: MJF Books, 2011.

Drury, Bob & Tom Clavin. *Valley Forge*. New York: Simon & Schuster. 2018.

Ellis, Joseph J. *Revolutionary Summer: The Birth of American Independence*. New York: Alfred A. Knopf, 2013.

———. *The Quartet: Orchestrating the Second American Revolution, 1783-1789*. New York: Alfred A. Knopf, 2015.

———. *His Excellency: George Washington*. New York: Alfred A. Knopf, 2004.

Flexner, James Thomas. *George Washington in the American Revolution, 1775-1783*. Boston: Little, Brown & Company, 1967.

Flower, Lenore Embick. "Visit of President George Washington to Carlisle, 1794." Carlisle, Pennsylvania: The Hamilton Library and Cumberland County Historical Society, 1932.

Gerlach, Don R. *Proud Patriot: Philip Schuyler and the War of Independence, 1775-1783*. Syracuse, N.Y.: Syracuse University Press, 1987.

Goodrich, Charles A. *Lives of the Signers of the Declaration of Independence*. Charlotteville, N.Y.: SamHar Press, 1976.

Griffith, IV, William R. *The Battle of Lake George: England's First Triumph in the French and Indian War*. Charleston, South Carolina: The History Press, 2016.

Grossman, Mark. *Encyclopedia of the Continental Congress*. Armenia, New York: Grey House Publishing, 2015.

Hamilton, Edward P. *Fort Ticonderoga: Key to a Continent*. Boston: Little, Brown & Company, 1964.

Isenberg, Nancy. *Fallen Founder: The Life of Aaron Burr*. New York: Penguin Group, 2007.

Kennedy, Roger G. *Burr, Hamilton, and Jefferson: A Study in Character*. New York: Oxford University Press, 1999.

Kiernan, Denise & Joseph D'Agnese. *Signing Their Lives Away: The Fame and Misfortune of the Men Who Signed the Declaration of Independence*. Philadelphia: Quirk Books, 2008.

———. *Signing Their Rights Away: The Fame and Misfortune of the Men Who Signed the United States Constitution*. Philadelphia: Quirk Books, 2011.

Klarman, Michael J. *The Framers' Coup: The Making of the United States Constitution*. New York: Oxford University Press, 2016.

Langguth, A. J. *Patriots*. New York: Simon and Schuster, 1988.

Larson, Edward J. *A Magnificent Catastrophe*. New York: Free Press, 2007.

Lee, Mike. Written *Out of History: The Forgotten Founders Who Fought Big Government*. New York: Penguin Books, 2017.

Lewis, James E., Jr., *The Burr Conspiracy: Uncovering the Story of an Early American Crisis*, Princeton: Princeton University Press, 2017.

Lockridge, Ross Franklin. *The Harrisons*. 1941.

Lomask, Milton. *Aaron Burr: The Years from Princeton to Vice President, 1756-1805*. New York: Farrar Straus Giroux, 1979.

Lossing, Benson J. *Pictorial Field Book of the Revolution*. New York: Harper Brothers. 1851.

Maier, Pauline. *American Scripture: Making the Declaration of Independence*. New York: Alfred A. Knopf, Inc., 1997.

McCullough, David. *John Adams*. New York: Simon & Schuster, 2002.

Meltzer, Brad & Josh Mensch. *The First Conspiracy: The Secret Plot to Kill George Washington*. New York: Flat Iron Books. 2018.

Middlekauff, Robert. *The Glorious Cause: The American Revolution, 1763-1789*. Oxford: Oxford University Press, 2005.

Miller, Jr., Arthur P. & Marjorie L. Miller. *Pennsylvania Battlefields and Military Landmarks*. Mechanicsburg, Pennsylvania: Stackpole Books, 2000.

Millett, Allan R. & Peter Maslowski. *For the Common Defense: A Military History of the United States of America*. New York: The Free Press, 1984.

Moore, Charles. *The Family Life of George Washington*. New York: Houghton Mifflin, 1926.

Nagel, Paul C. *The Lees of Virginia: Seven Generations of an American Family*. Oxford: Oxford University Press, 1990.

O'Connell, Robert L. *Revolutionary: George Washington at War*. New York: Random House. 2019.

Racove, Jack N. *Revolutionaries: A New History of the Invention of America*. New York: Houghton Mifflin Harcourt, 2011.

Raphael, Ray. Founding Myths: *Stories That Hide Our Patriotic Past*. New York: MJF Books, 2004.

Rossiter, Clinton. *1787 The Grand Convention*. New York: The Macmillan Company, 1966.

Seymour, Joseph. *The Pennsylvania Associators, 1747-1777*. Yardley, Pennsylvania: Westholme Publishing, LLC. 2012.

Schweikart, Larry & Michael Allen. *A Patriot's History of the United States from Columbus's Great Discovery to the War on Terror*. New York: Penguin, 2004.

Sharp, Arthur G. *Not Your Father's Founders*. Avon, Massachusetts: Adams Media, 2012.

Stahr, Walter. *John Jay: Founding Father*. New York: Diversion Books, 2017.

Taafee, Stephen R. *The Philadelphia Campaign, 1777-1778*. Lawrence, Kansas: University of Kansas Press, 2003.

Tinkcom, Harry Marlin, *The Republicans and the Federalists in Pennsylvania, 1790-1801*. Harrisburg, Pennsylvania: Pennsylvania Historical and Museum Commission. 1950.

Ward, Matthew C. *Breaking the Backcountry: The Seven Years' War in Virginia and Pennsylvania, 1754-1765*. Pittsburgh, Pennsylvania: University of Pittsburgh Press, 2003.

Weisberger, Bernard A. *America Afire: Jefferson, Adams, and the Revolutionary Election of 1800*. New York: HarperCollins, 2000.

Wood, Gordon S. *The Radicalism of the American Revolution*. New York: Vintage Books, 1993.

———. *Empire of Liberty: A History of the Early Republic, 1789-1815*. New York: Penguin Books, 2004.

———. *Revolutionary Characters: What Made the Founders Different*. New York: Penguin Books, 2006.

SOURCES

———. *The Americanization of Benjamin Franklin*. Oxford: Oxford University Press, 2009.

Wright, Benjamin F. *The Federalist: The Famous Papers on the Principles of American Government: Alexander Hamilton, James Madison, John Jay*. New York: Metro Books, 2002.

Zobel, Hiller B. *The Boston Massacre*. New York: W. W. Norton & Company, 1970.

Video Resources:

Guelzo, Allen C. The Great Courses: *America's Founding Fathers* (Course N. 8525). Chantilly, Virginia: The Teaching Company, 2017.

Online Resources:

Archives.gov – for information on the Constitutional Convention.

CauseofLiberty.blogspot.com – for information on Daniel Carroll.

ColonialHall.com – for information about the signers of the Declaration of Independence.

DSDI1776.com – for information on many Founders.

FamousAmericans.net – for information on many Founders.

FindaGrave.com – for burial information, vital statistics and obituaries.

FirstLadies.org – for information on Abigail Adams.

Newspapers.com – Hundreds of newspaper articles were accessed—too numerous to mention here.

NPS.gov – for information on various park sites.

TeachingAmericanHistory.com – for information on Charles Pinckney and George Wythe.

TheHistoryJunkie.com – for information on multiple Founders.

USHistory.org – for information on multiple Founders.

Wikipedia.com – for general historical information.

Index

INDEX

INDEX